The Book of
SCENES for
ACTING PRACTICE

Marshall Cassady

National Textbook Company
a division of NTC *Publishing Group*

To Martha Hildenbrand

1991 Printing

Published by National Textbook Company, a division of NTC Publishing Group,
© 1985 by NTC Publishing Group, 4255 West Touhy Avenue,
Lincolnwood (Chicago), Illinois 60646-1975 U.S.A.
Manufactured in the United States of America.
Library of Congress Catalog Number: 84-61516

0 ML 9 8 7

Acknowledgments

Excerpts from:

Antigone by Jean Anouilh, translated by Lewis Galantiere. Copyright 1946 by Random House, Inc. and renewed 1974 by Lewis Galantiere. Reprinted by permission of the publisher.

The Bald Soprano by Eugene Ionesco, translated by Donald M. Allen in *Four Plays by Eugene Ionesco,* copyright © 1956, 1965 by Grove Press, Inc. Reprinted by permission of the publisher.

Barefoot in the Park by Neil Simon. Copyright © 1964 by Ellen Enterprises, Inc. Reprinted by permission of Random House, Inc.

Blithe Spirit by Noel Coward. Copyright © 1941 by Noel Coward. Reprinted by permission of Doubleday, Inc.

The Diary of Anne Frank by Frances Goodrich and Albert Hackett. Copyright 1954, 1956 as an unpublished work. Copyright © by Albert Hackett, Frances Goodrich and Otto Frank. Reprinted by permission of Random House, Inc.

The Glass Menagerie by Tennessee Williams. Copyright 1945 by Tennessee Williams and Edwina C. Williams and renewed 1973 by Tennessee Williams. Reprinted by permission of Random House, Inc.

The Late Christopher Bean by Sidney Howard. Reprint permission by Brandt & Brandt Literary Agency, Inc. © 1932 (under title, *Muse of All Work*) by Sidney Howard, copyright 1933 by Sidney Howard, Copyright 1959, 1960 in renewal by Dolly Damrosch Howard. All rights reserved.

The Lion in Winter by James Goldman. Copyright © 1964 by James Goldman as an unpublished work. Copyright © 1966 by James Goldman. Reprinted by permission of Random House, Inc.

Long Day's Journey Into Night by Eugene O'Neill. Copyright 1955 by Carlotta Monterey O'Neill. Renewed 1983 by Oona O'Neill Chaplin and Yale University Press.

The Miser, translated by Sylvan Barnet, Morton Berman, and William Burto, first appeared in their edition of *Eight Great Comedies,* published by the New American Library. Copyright 1958 by Sylvan Barnet, Morton Berman, and William Burto.

CONTENTS

Introduction

I n *The Book of Scenes for Acting Practice* drama students will find a variety of compelling scenes for acting practice. The scenes presented here were chosen to represent a variety of historical periods and styles. Ranging from the Elizabethan period to the current, from Shakespeare's blank verse tragedy to the modern slang of the streets, they present compelling moments from important plays.

Elaborate sets are not needed to convey the feeling and mood of each scene. Nor do most of the scenes require more than basic properties. For example, Jaques's monologue from Shakespeare's *As You Like It* does not need a forest clearing to be effective. A bare acting space does not detract from the glorious language in that scene. All of the scenes presented here were chosen with simplicity and ease of presentation in mind. Actors who prefer to wear special costumes and makeup certainly may do so, but it isn't necessary. The scenes can be effectively presented without them.

In addition to period and style, the user of *The Book of Scenes for Acting Practice* will find a great variety of character types. Students thus have a chance to try out many different stage personalities. Playing different character types helps actors learn about human nature and about themselves. Analyzing the characters and attempting to understand them can provide insights into human behavior, a strong asset in any future roles the actor may attempt.

Introductions to the scenes give the time, setting, and general background necessary for understanding the characters. The scenes themselves have been chosen so that with little explanation they can make sense by themselves. Questions provided with each scene aid in the interpretation of roles and the staging of the action.

These scenes are intended for students to practice in order to grow in skill and understanding. They are not intended for polished performances before an audience. With their depth and variety, the scenes give students opportunities to gain insights into human life and behavior and to join with others in creating the magic of theatre. Good luck!

PREPARING THE SCENES

The scenes in *The Book of Scenes for Acting Practice* were chosen to give you a chance to interpret and act in a variety of plays from ancient Greek times to the present. Before presenting any of them, it is best to read the play from which each is taken. In this way you can see how the scene fits into the overall play and get a better idea of what each character is like.

Then analyze what you have read. After you determine the direction of the action and what your character is like, you then have a basis for determining how to play a scene.

Analyzing the Play

Understanding a play involves a number of steps. You can develop your overall understanding by answering the following questions:

1. What do you know about the playwright? When and where did he or she live? How did environment and background affect what each wrote? What had the most affect on the writing?

2. What is the play about? Every play has a major theme or central idea the author wants to convey to an audience. What is the theme of the play? How does it affect the progression of the action and the type of characters that are included?

3. How is the play structured? Where are the high and low points? What type of drama is it? Is it comic or tragic? The drama type will have an influence on how you portray the characters. For example, comedy usually has a broader or more exaggerated style than does a serious play.

4. What are the circumstances of time and place? Where does the action take place? What is it like there? Is it like or unlike the world in which we live? Are there special social or economic conditions that affect the characters?

Answering these questions leads to an understanding of the play as a whole. With such an understanding, it's easier to concentrate on an individual scene and its characters.

Analyzing Your Scene

Ask yourself similar questions to analyze your scene. You need to know:

1. Where are the high points of the action and what are the most important lines? This can help you plan the blocking and movement to emphasize ideas and speeches.

2. How do the characters interact with each other? What kinds of relationships do they have? What are their psychological and emotional ties?

A playwright's purpose always should be to present truth as he or she sees it. This means that the actor needs to understand how the playwright views life and then be true to this view in the portrayal of character.

Analyzing Your Character

You need to be even more detailed and exacting in analyzing the character you will play. You can begin with those things that the playwright has stated or suggested both in the character description and in the character's own lines as well as the lines of others. But this is only the starting point. Think about the character. Try to imagine how the character thinks and feels.

Your interpretation may be different from that of another actor playing the scene, but that is all right so long as you can justify what you do in light of the rest of the play. No two actors interpret a character exactly alike. This is what makes theatre interesting. We begin to develop a character with what the playwright has provided. But we go on much further, adding what we think fits in with the total personality.

There is no particular order that is best in analyzing a character, but it might be easiest to begin with the most concrete aspects—the physical traits. These are of two types, the ones over which the actor has little control, such as height and weight, and those which can be altered. These include dress, hair style and so forth. The more complete you can make the physical picture, generally the more real the character becomes to you as an actor.

Questions about character include:

1. What is the character's background? What kind of education does he or she have? What sort of family does he or she come from?

Where did the character grow up and later live? What has played the biggest part in shaping the character's personality?

2. What are the character's interests? What kind of work does the character do or want to do? Why? How does he or she like to spend free time? If the character has a house or apartment, how is it furnished? Why?

3. What character traits are evident? How does the character impress other people? Is he or she generally happy or unhappy? What are the most important aspects of his or her personality? What are the dominant traits? What kind of friends does she or he have?

4. How does the character feel about others? About self? About the world in general?

After you have determined all you think you need to know, how does what you learned affect your portrayal of the person? For instance, how does she or he speak? Is it slow and deliberate or staccato and rapid? What makes this so?

Of course you can think of many other questions in addition to those mentioned here. You should know much more about your character than you ever need tell the audience and much more than is mentioned in the script. This helps make the person real and the actions more believable.

It is good practice to write out your analysis so you can determine if there are any gaps in the interpretation. You may want to write the analysis out in paragraph form or use a format similar to the following:

Character Analysis

Play _____

Playwright _____

Scene _____

My Character _____

My Character's Background:

    A. Social

    B. Educational

C. Geographic

D. Family

E. Major Influences

F. Environment (time and place)

Interests:
   A. Jobs

   B. Hobbies

   C. Friends

   D. Other Spare-Time Activities

Personality Traits:

Relationship with Other Characters:

Goals:

Playwright's Life and Influences on Writing the Play:

Theme and Meaning of the Play:

Brief Description of the Other Characters:

Monologues
for Women

Long Day's Journey into Night

The Late Christopher Bean

The Bald Soprano

Act 3

Lonq Day's Journey into Niqht

Eugene O'Neill

This is an autobiographical play that recalls the relationships among the members of the Tyrone family: James, the father; Mary, the mother; and Jamie and Edmund, the sons. The characters are based on O'Neill's own family and are so true-to-life that the author did not want the play produced until after his death. The action takes place in the Tyrones' summer home. The time is 1912.

Each of the four main characters is unhappy. Tyrone regrets that he didn't make more of his life and become a great actor, particularly since he had the potential to do so. Instead he chose to take a role in a popular melodrama, which would be comparable today to a great actor appearing in a long running soap opera. Edmund, based on Eugene O'Neill, has tuberculosis and will soon have to enter a sanitarium. Jamie, the oldest son, is an alcoholic, and Mary has become addicted to morphine as a result of being treated by a quack doctor.

Because her life is unhappy, Mary often retreats into her past. The monologue that follows contains clues about her character. Most important, perhaps, is that she is a romantic, as we see in the description of her first encounter with James Tyrone. Mary is lonely and has no friends with whom she can discuss her problems. Therefore, she talks to Cathleen, the maid, even though she realizes that one would not usually talk to a servant about such personal things. The action occurs in the living room of the family's summer home. In the center of the room is a round table surrounded by four chairs—three wicker armchairs and a varnished oak rocker.

MARY: If you think Mr. Tyrone is handsome now, Cathleen, you should have seen him when I first met him. He had the reputation of being one of the best looking men in the country. The girls in the Convent who had seen him act, or seen his photographs, used to rave about him. He was a great matinee idol then, you know. Women used to wait at the stage door just to see him come out. You can imagine how excited I was when my father wrote me he and James Tyrone had become friends, and that I was to meet him when I came home for Easter vacation. I showed the letter to all the girls, and how envious they were! My father took me to see him act first. It was a play about the French Revolution and the leading part was a nobleman. I couldn't take my eyes off him. I wept when he was thrown in prison—and then was so mad at myself because I was afraid my eyes and nose would be red. My father said we'd go backstage to his dressing room right after the play, and so we did. [*She gives a little excited, shy laugh.*] I was so bashful all I could do was stammer and blush like a little fool. But he didn't seem to think I was a fool. I know he liked me the first moment we were introduced. [*Coquettishly.*] I guess my eyes and nose couldn't have been red, after all. I was really very pretty then, Cathleen. And he was handsomer than my wildest dream, in his make-up and his nobleman's costume that was so becoming to him. He was different from all ordinary men, like someone from another world. At the same time he was simple, and kind, and unassuming, not a bit stuck-up or vain. I fell in love right then. So did he, he told me afterwards. I forgot all about becoming a nun or a concert pianist. All I wanted was to be his wife. [*She pauses, staring before her with unnaturally bright, dreamy eyes, and a rapt, tender, girlish smile.*] Thirty-six years ago, but I can see it as clearly as if it were tonight! We've loved each other ever since. And in all those thirty-six years, there has never been a breath of scandal about him. I mean, with any other woman. Never since he met me. That has made me very happy, Cathleen. It has made me forgive so many other things.

Interpretation

1. People who have a romantic outlook on life often are unrealistic in the way they view the past. They often think things more beautiful or exciting than they really are. What specific words in Mary's reminiscence show she is romanticizing the first meeting with James Tyrone? How might you point up these words for an audience?

2. Mary's statement that her husband's "faithfulness" has made her very happy is an overstatement. Why do you think she finds it necessary to exaggerate this feeling?

3. Mary is a very lonely person. What clues can you find in the lines that show this?

4. Mary is addicted to morphine and lives in a romanticized past. What movements could you have her make to convey the type of person she is? What clothes might she wear to convey her personality?

5. What emotions does Mary feel in this scene? What lines show her feelings? How can you logically portray these emotions to an audience?

Act 2

The Late Christopher Bean

Sidney Howard

This play is an American folk comedy with Yankee (New England) characters. Using humor to criticize human nature, the play focuses on greed. Christopher Bean, an artist who lived with a physician and his family, has been proclaimed a genius ten years after his death. Now people are flocking to the physician's home to buy paintings that he may have left there. Each of the characters, except Abby, is overcome with greed at the thought of the money now to be made from the paintings. She remains a simple, honest woman, still devoted to Christopher's memory. She has been a servant to Dr. Haggett's family for the past fifteen years.

Just before this monologue another character, Tallant, asks Abby what Chris taught her. Tallant is an art forger who wants to persuade the physician to agree with his scheme to forge paintings and pass them off as Bean's. The following is Abby's answer to Tallant's question. She speaks in her characteristic Yankee twang. The set is described by the author as "the dining room of an old house in a New England Village."

ABBY: [*only too eager to tell*] Oh, I remember! It was mostly things to see, I guess. Like the rust color the marshes get this time of year when the sky gets the color of that old blue platter. [*She points to the platter on the cabinet shelf, adding proudly*] That's cobalt blue! That's a painting term, cobalt blue! [*She continues.*] And he showed me the old red barn and the covered bridge that he was forever painting and I was used to all my life and never noticed. And he taught me that old chairs may be more than just old chairs to be thrown away. That some of 'em may be real beautiful. He used to say them very words about the old doors in the brick houses up along the common! That was when they began taking the old doors out and putting in new ones ordered from Sears Roebuck. And did you know that old brick houses ain't red but mostly green and brown and that moonlight and snow ain't white at all but all kinds of colors and that elm trees is most decorative when their leaves comes off? That's another painting term, decorative. He taught me! [*Her reminiscence becomes more personal.*] He taught me that a man can get drunk and not be no different only just more so and that everybody's got more good qualities than bad. Oh, he taught me lots! And I ain't never forgot none of it. I lived over and over that time he spent here. Over and over it ever since he died.

Interpretation

1. It is established at the end of the play that Abby really is Christopher's widow; she has kept her marriage a secret. But she is proud of having been taught about painting by Chris. What are the other, perhaps more important things, he taught her about human nature? Show the specific line that reveals this attitude toward other people. How would you point up this line?

2. What do you think is the mood of the last two sentences of this monologue? Why has Abby lived over and over in her mind what Christopher told her? What emotion would you try to convey to the audience with these lines?

3. Abby is not an artist and never has been. Why then do you think she remembers so much about painting? How do you think she feels about art? Name at least three things about art that she does know. What mood would you try to establish in playing Abby and in presenting her knowledge to an audience?

4. The stage directions say that her recollections become more personal at a certain point. What does this mean? How does her

reminiscence change? How might you convey, through voice or movement, this transition from impersonal to personal?

5. Why do you think the stage directions say Abby is "only too eager to tell" Tallant what Chris taught her? In what way could you portray this eagerness? Through rate of speaking? Vocal quality? Movement?

6. What in the monologue shows that Abby loves Christopher? How would you portray this love?

7. The monologue shows that Abby views life positively and optimistically. How can these traits be pointed up for an audience?

The Bald Soprano

Eugene Ionesco

This play is an example of Theatre of the Absurd. This does not mean the play itself is absurd. The name indicates that playwrights who wrote in this style considered life to be absurd. In their plays they attempted to present life's absurdity without making any comment on it. In other words, they didn't suggest, through their writing, that life should be changed. They simply presented the truth as they saw it.

According to Ionesco, the setting is a "middle-class English interior, with English armchairs. An English evening. Mr. Smith, an Englishman, seated in his English armchair and wearing English slippers, is smoking his English pipe and reading an English newspaper near an English fire. He is wearing English spectacles and a small gray English moustache. Beside him, in another English armchair, Mrs. Smith, an Englishwoman, is darning some English socks. A long moment of English silence. The English clock strikes 17 English strokes."

This scene opens the play and immediately sets the tone for what is to follow. There are two main ideas presented here. The first is that people really don't talk about anything that is important. Mrs. Smith rattles on, often not even making sense. Her actions and reactions often don't seem to be related to what she actually says. Second, Mr. Smith, during this portion of the opening scene, hardly reacts at all. It is apparent that he is paying no attention to what his wife is saying. Instead, it's as if he's placed his mind on "automatic drive" where his wife is concerned. His responses are not related to her dialogue. Of course, she isn't paying attention to him either, so she doesn't respond to his lack of interest in her conversation.

MRS. SMITH: There, it's nine o'clock. We've drunk the soup, and eaten the fish and chips, and the English salad. The children have drunk English water. We've eaten well this evening. That's because we live in the suburbs of London and because our name is Smith.

MR. SMITH: [*continues to read, clicks his tongue.*]

MRS. SMITH: Potatoes are very good fried in fat; the salad oil was not rancid. The oil from the grocer at the corner is better quality than the oil from the grocer across the street. It is even better than the oil from the grocer at the bottom of the street. However, I prefer not to tell them that their oil is bad.

MR. SMITH: [*continues to read, clicks his tongue.*]

MRS. SMITH: However, the oil from the grocer at the corner is still the best.

MR. SMITH: [*continues to read, clicks his tongue.*]

MRS. SMITH: Mary did the potatoes very well, this evening. The last time she did not do them well. I do not like them when they are well done.

MR. SMITH: [*continues to read, clicks his tongue.*]

MRS. SMITH: The fish was fresh. It made my mouth water. I had two helpings. No, three helpings. That made me go to the w.c. You also had three helpings. However, the third time you took less than the first two times, while as for me, I took a great deal more. I eat better than you this evening. Why is that? Usually, it is you who eats more. It is not appetite you lack.

MR. SMITH: [*clicks his tongue.*]

MRS. SMITH: But still, the soup was perhaps a little too salt. It was saltier than you. Ha, ha, ha. It also had too many leeks and not enough onions. I regret I didn't advise Mary to add some aniseed stars. The next time I'll know better.

MR. SMITH: [*continues to read, clicks his tongue.*]

MRS. SMITH: Our little boy wanted to drink some beer; he's going to love getting tiddly. He's like you. At table did you notice how he stared at the bottle? But I poured some water from the jug into his glass. He was thirsty and he drank it. Helen is like me: she's a good manager, thrifty, plays the piano. She never asks to drink English beer. She's like our little daughter who drinks only milk and eats only porridge. It's obvious that she's only two. She's named Peggy. The quince and bean pie was marvelous. It would have been nice, perhaps, to have had a small glass of Australian Burgundy with the sweet, but I did not bring the bottle to the table because I did not wish to set the children a bad example of gluttony. They must learn to be sober and temperate.

MR. SMITH: [*continues to read, clicks his tongue.*]

MRS. SMITH: Mrs. Parker knows a Rumanian grocer by the Name of Popesco Rosenfeld, who has just come from Constantinople. He is a great specialist in yogurt. He has a diploma from the school of yogurt-making in Adrianople. Tomorrow I shall buy a large pot of native Rumanian yogurt from him. One doesn't often find such things here in the suburbs of London.

MR. SMITH: [*continues to read, clicks his tongue.*]

MRS. SMITH: Yogurt is excellent for the stomach, the kidneys, the appendicitis, and apotheosis. It was Doctor Mackenzie-King who told me that, he's the one who takes care of the children of our neighbors, the Johns. He's a good doctor. One can trust him. He never prescribes any medicine that he's not tried out on himself first. Before operating on Parker, he had his own liver operated on first, although he was not the least bit ill.

Interpretation

1. Since one of the ideas the author wants to bring out in *The Bald Soprano* is that people pay little attention to one another, how might you have Mrs. Smith indicate she is speaking to her husband, yet paying little attention to him?

2. Mrs. Smith is described by Ionesco as typically English. How might you convey this idea?

3. Since Mrs. Smith's actions don't relate to what she's saying, what might you have her do in this scene?

4. What tone of voice or vocal quality would be appropriate for this scene? Why?

5. How do you visualize Mrs. Smith's physical appearance? How would you want to change your own appearance to fit the character?

6. Why does Mrs. Smith go on and on about the dinner and the food? What emotions does she feel when she does this? How might you communicate these emotions to an audience?

7. Why does Mrs. Smith change subjects so quickly? Do people do this in real life?

8. Some of what Mrs. Smith says is obvious nonsense. List at least five examples of such lines. What tone of voice or emotion might be appropriate for each of these?

Monologues
for Men

You're a Good Man, Charlie Brown

Long Day's Journey Into Night

As You Like It

Long Day's Journey into Night
Photo by C. James Gleason
Courtesy of Kent State University
Theatre, Kent, Ohio

Act 1

You're a Good Man, Charlie Brown

Clark Gesner

This musical is based on the *Peanuts* comic strip by Charles
Schultz. Anyone familiar with *Peanuts* knows that Charlie
Brown is a born loser who can't seem to succeed at anything he
tries. He's the self-conscious butt of many jokes. The other kids,
Lucy, in particular, try to take advantage of his good nature and
trust.

Usually, when the play is presented, no attempt is made to
make the characters appear like those in the comic strip. The set
is not at all realistic. Platforms and three-dimensional, geometric
shapes are used to suggest where the action takes place. Also, the
play does not follow one story line throughout but is a series of
vignettes.

CHARLIE BROWN: I think lunchtime is about the worst time of
the day for me. Always having to sit here alone. Of
course, sometimes mornings aren't so pleasant, either—
waking up and wondering if anyone would really miss me if I
never got out of bed. Then there's the night, too—lying there
and thinking about all the stupid things I've done during the
day. And all those hours in between—when I do all those
stupid things. Well, lunchtime is *among* the worst times of
the day for me.

Well, I guess I'd better see what I've got. [*He opens the
bag, unwraps a sandwich, and looks inside.*] Peanut
butter. [*He bites and chews.*] Some psychiatrists say that
people who eat peanut butter sandwiches are lonely. I
guess they're right. And if you're really lonely, the
peanut butter sticks to the roof of your mouth. [*He*

munches quietly, idly fingering the bench.] Boy, the PTA sure did a good job of painting these benches. [*He looks off to one side.*] There's that cute little redheaded girl eating her lunch over there. I wonder what she'd do if I went over and asked her if I could sit and have lunch with her. She'd probably laugh right in my face. It's hard on a face when it gets laughed in. There's an empty place next to her on the bench. There's no reason why I couldn't just go over and sit there. I could do that right now. All I have to do is stand up. [*He stands.*] I'm standing up. [*He sits.*] I'm sitting down. I'm a coward. I'm so much of a coward she wouldn't even think of looking at me. She hardly ever *does* look at me. In fact, I can't remember her ever looking at me. Why shouldn't she look at me? Is there any reason in the world why she shouldn't look at me? Is she so great and am I so small that she couldn't spare one little moment just to . . . [*He freezes.*] She's looking at me. [*In terror he looks one way, then another.*] She's *looking* at me. [*His head looks all around, frantically trying to find something else to notice. His teeth clench. Tension builds. Then, with one motion, he pops the paper bag over his head.* LUCY *and* PATTY *enter.*]

Interpretation

1. What actions would be appropriate in the first paragraph of this monologue? Keep in mind the well known instructions to actors to suit the action to the words and the words to the action.

2. Since the play is usually done with a set made up of platforms and shapes and performers who are much older than the characters they depict, how could you let the audience "see" where the action takes place?

3. What things does Charlie say in the scene that reveal the type of person he is?

4. What is Charlie's posture in this scene? How would his posture help reveal his personality?

5. When the redheaded girl looks at Charlie, he is terrified. How would you show his feelings through his movements and facial expression?

6. Do you think Charlie will ever get up enough nerve to sit by or talk to the redheaded girl? Why or why not?

7. If you could help Charlie feel better, how would you do it?

8. Charlie wants the redheaded girl to notice him. Yet the thought of her doing so terrifies him. How can you portray both of these feelings simultaneously?

9. How would you have Charlie move in order to portray his character?

Act 4

Lonq Day's Journey iNTo NiqHT

Eugene O'Neill

J ust as you saw with Mary, each member of the Tyrone family
has a monologue revealing feelings and character (See
page 3 for further background.) Here Edmund has just listened to
his father, James Tyrone, talk about how difficult his life has
been and how he had the talent to be a first-rate actor. Instead,
he chose to play a continuing role in a popular play, *The Count of
Monte Cristo.* The public thought of him only as a second-rate
actor, and he felt his talent was wasted.

Edmund has learned that he has tuberculosis and will have to
enter a sanitarium. The year is 1912. He and his father are
sitting at the dining room table.

E DMUND: You've just told me some· high spots in your memories. Want to hear mine? They're all connected with the
sea. Here's one. When I was on the *Squarehead* square
rigger, bound for Buenos Aires. Full moon in the Trades.
The old hooker driving fourteen knots. I lay on the
bowsprit, facing astern, with the water foaming into
spume under me, the masts with every sail white in the
moonlight towering high above me. I became drunk with
the beauty and singing rhythm of it, and for a moment I
lost myself—actually lost my life. I was set free! I
became beauty and rhythm, became moonlight and the
ship and the high dim-starred sky! I belonged without past
or future, within peace and unity and a wild joy, within
something greater than my own life, or the life of Man,

to Life itself! To God, if you want to put it that way. Then another time, on the American Line, when I was lookout on the crow's nest in the dawn watch. A calm sea, that time. Only a lazy ground swell and a slow drowsy roll of the ship. The passengers asleep and none of the crew in sight. No sound of man. Black smoke pouring from the funnels behind and beneath me. Dreaming, not keeping lookout, feeling alone, and above, and apart, watching the dawn creep like a painted dream over the sky and sea which slept together. When the moment of ecstatic freedom came. The peace, the end of the quest, the last harbor, the joy of belonging to a fulfillment beyond man's lousy, pitiful, greedy fears and hopes and dreams! And several other times of my life, when I was swimming far out, or lying alone on a beach, I have had the same experience. Became the sun, the hot sand, green seaweed anchored to a rock, swaying in the tide. Like a saint's vision of beatitude. Like the veil of things as they seem drawn back by an unseen hand. For a second you see—and seeing the secret, are the secret. For a second there is meaning! Then the hand lets the veil fall and you are alone, lost in the fog again, and you stumble on toward nowhere, for no good reason. [*He grins wryly.*] It was a great mistake, my being born a man. I would have been much more successful as a seagull or a fish. As it is, I will always be a stranger who never feels at home, who does not really want and is not really wanted, who can never belong, who must always be a little in love with death!

Interpretation

1. Edmund reacts to his father's regrets about wasting his talent as an actor. Then he tells his own experiences at sea, recalling special moments. What is his predominant mood as he talks? How would you convey this mood to an audience?

2. What tone of voice would you use to convey Edmund's enthusiasm for the sea?

3. Often people move around when they are caught up in what they are saying, when they want to emphasize something or get their ideas across, and when they switch from one idea to

another. Pick out the times when some of these things occur in Edmund's speech. What sorts of movement would you have him make at these points?

4. Gestures emphasize and describe. Select at least three places when either type of gesture might be used.

5. Describe how Edmund might dress to reveal the type of person he is.

6. For Edmund the sea has a very special quality. What is this quality?

AS YOU LIKE IT

William Shakespeare

This delightful play is based on a novel by Thomas Lodge and has many characteristics of a pastoral romance, meaning a piece of writing that has to do with the countryside and rural characters. In the story the wicked Duke Frederick has seized the throne from his brother, Duke Senior, who has retreated to the forest where he lives like Robin Hood. Later Frederick also exiles his niece, Rosiland, from court. She and a friend, Celia, disguise themselves and set out to find Duke Senior. Orlando, who has fallen in love with Rosiland, also must flee, because he has angered his elder brother Oliver. Ultimately, Orlando and Rosiland marry, as do several other couples, including Oliver and Celia. Then Duke Frederick repents his wrongdoing and welcomes Duke Senior back to court.

Jaques, who delivers the well-known monologue given here, is one of Duke Senior's followers. Although he contributes nothing to the plot, Jaques is a well-developed character. Most often in story plays (those that have a plot) only the major characters whose actions have a direct bearing on the plot, are fully developed. It is possible that Shakespeare developed the character so well in order to give the role to a particular member of his acting company.

The monologue is delivered at the banished Duke's headquarters in the forest and seems to have little bearing on what has preceded it in the dialogue, except that the Duke remarks to Jaques: "Thou seest we are not all alone unhappy: this wide and universal theatre presents more woeful pageants than the scene wherein we play in."

JAQUES: All the world's a stage,
　　　　And all the men and women merely players:
　　　　They have their exits and their entrances;

And one man in his time plays many parts,
His acts being seven ages. At first the infant,
Mewling[1] and puking in the nurse's arms.
And then the whining school-boy, with his satchel
And shining morning face, creeping like snail
Unwillingly to school. And then the lover,
Sighing like furnace, with a woeful ballad
Made to his mistress' eyebrow. Then a soldier,
Full of strange oaths and bearded like the pard,[2]
Jealous in honour, sudden and quick in quarrel,
Seeking the bubble reputation[3]
Even in the cannon's mouth.[4] And then the justice,
In fair round belly with good capon lined,[5]
With eyes severe and beard of formal cut,
Full of wise saws[6] and modern instances[7]
And so he plays his part. The sixth age shifts
Into the lean and slipper'd pantaloon,[8]
With spectacles on nose and pouch on side,
His youthful hose, well saved, a world too wide
For his shrunk shank; and his big manly voice,
Turning again toward childish treble, pipes
And whistles in his sound. Last scene of all,
That ends this strange eventful history,
In second childishness and mere oblivion,
Sans teeth, sans eyes, sans taste, sans everything.

Interpretation

1. Jaques takes a very mocking attitude toward each stage of
life he describes. List each of the seven instances of this. In what
way could you use your voice to emphasize and convey each of
these seven ideas?

2. In production this scene is often delivered directly to an
audience. What movement from place to place might be made in
delivering the monologue to an audience? When should these
movements occur?

[1]feeble [2]leopard [3]fleeting fame [4]as a soldier [5]full of good food
obtained through bribes [6]wise sayings [7]commonplace illustrations
[8]feeble old man

3. Posture and body carriage can help convey character. For instance, a weary or old person might move slowly and be stooped over. A person who is angry might make stiff, angular movements. How would you have Jaques carry himself to convey what he's like?

4. As an actor playing Jaques, what feelings would you try to elicit from an audience with this monologue? How would you go about doing this?

5. Shakespeare's plays are often difficult to understand because of the language and style. To be sure you understand the meaning of this scene write it out in your own words.

6. How old do you think Jacques is? What makes you think so? How would you suggest his age?

SCENES FOR TWO WOMEN

ROMEO AND JULIET

BLITHE SPIRIT

THE GLASS MENAGERIE

THE LION IN WINTER

THE IMPORTANCE OF BEING EARNEST

Act 2, scene 5

ROMEO AND JULIET

William Shakespeare

This play is considered by many to be one of the greatest love stories of all time. Although older performers usually play the roles, Juliet is only fourteen and Romeo sixteen. Each is from opposite sides of an ancient and ongoing family feud; Romeo is a Montague and Juliet a Capulet. They meet at a masked ball given by the Capulets. Romeo has been persuaded by a friend, Benvolio, to attend in order to compare Rosaline, whom he thinks he loves, with the girls there. Of course, this is where he and Juliet fall in love.

This scene occurs the day after Romeo and Juliet agree to a secret marriage. Juliet has sent her nurse to make final arrangements for the wedding which is to occur at Friar Lawrence's cell, a small religious house near a monastery. The friar, Romeo's friend, hopes that the couple's love for each other will result in an end to the family feud. As the directions indicate, the action occurs outdoors, in Capulet's orchard.

JULIET: The clock struck nine when I did send the nurse.
In half an hour she promised to return.
Perchance she cannot meet him. That's not so.
Oh, she is lame! Love's heralds should be thoughts,
Which ten times faster glide than the sun's beams,
Driving back shadows over lowering[1] hills.
Therefore do nimble-pinioned[2] doves draw love,
And therefore hath the wind-swift Cupid wings.
Now is the sun upon the highmost hill
Of this day's journey, and from nine till twelve

---

[1]frowning [2]swift-winged doves were said to draw the chariot of Venus, goddess of love

Is three long hours; yet she is not come.
Had she affections and warm youthful blood,
She would be as swift in motion as a ball,
My words would bandy³ her to my sweet love,
And his to me.
But old folks; many feign as they were dead,
Unwieldy, slow, heavy and pale as lead,
[*Enter* NURSE, *with* PETER.] Oh, God, she comes! O
honey Nurse, what news?
Hast thou met with him? Send thy man away.

NURSE: Peter, stay at the gate.   [*Exit* PETER.]

JULIET: Now, good sweet Nurse—Oh, Lord, why look'st thou
sad?
Though news be sad, yet tell them merrily;
If good, thou shamest the music of sweet news
By playing it to me with so sour a face.

NURSE: I am aweary, give me leave⁴ a while.
Fie, how my bones ache! What a jaunce⁵ have I had!

JULIET: I would thou hadst my bones and I thy news.
Nay, come, I pray thee, speak, good, good Nurse, speak.

NURSE: Jesu, what haste? Can you not stay a while?
Do you not see that I am out of breath?

JULIET: How art thou out of breath when thou hast breath
To say to me that thou art out of breath?
The excuse that thou dost make in this delay
Is longer than the tale thou dost excuse.
Is thy news good, or bad? Answer to that.
Say either, and I'll stay the circumstance.⁶
Let me be satisfied, is't good or bad?

NURSE: Well, you have made a simple choice. You
know not how to choose a man. Romeo! No, not he,
Though his face be better than any man's yet his
leg excels all men's; and for a hand, and a foot, and a
body, though they be not to be talked on, yet they
are past compare. He is not the flower of courtesy,⁷
but, I'll warrant him, as gentle as a lamb. Go thy
ways, wench, serve God. What, have you dined at home?

---

³hit back and forth, as in tennis   ⁴let me be by myself   ⁵running
back and forth   ⁶wait for details   ⁷perfect gentleman

JULIET: No, no. But all this did I know before.
What says he of our marriage? What of that?

NURSE: Lord, how my head aches! What a head have I!
It beats as it would fall in twenty pieces.
My back o't other side—ah, my back, my back!
Beshrew[8] your heart for sending me about
To catch my death with jauncing up and down!

JULIET: I' faith, I am sorry that thou are not well.
Sweet, sweet, sweet Nurse, tell me, what says my love?

NURSE: Your love says, like an honest gentleman,
and a courteous, and a kind, and a handsome, and, I
warrant, a virtuous—Where is your mother?

JULIET: Where is my mother! Why, she is within,
Where should she be? How oddly thou repliest!
"Your love says, like an honest gentleman,
Where is your mother?"

NURSE: Oh, God's Lady dear!
Are you so hot?[9] Marry, come up,[10] I trow.
Is this the poultice for my aching bones?
Henceforward do your messages yourself.

JULIET: Here's such a coil![11] Come, what says Romeo?

NURSE: Have you got leave to go to shrift today?

JULIET: I have.

NURSE: Then hie[12] you hence to Friar Laurence' cell,
There stays a husband to make you a wife.
Now comes the wanton blood up in your cheeks,
They'll be in scarlet straight at any news.
Hie you to church, I must another way,
To fetch a ladder by the which your love
Must climb a bird's nest soon when it is dark.
I am the drudge, and toil in your delight,
But you shall bear the burden soon at night.
Go, I'll to dinner, hie you to the cell.

JULIET: Hie to high fortune! Honest Nurse, farewell.

[*Exeunt.*]

[8]a curse on bad luck [9]eager [10]a slang expression similar to "go on" [11]fuss [12]hurry

Interpretation

1. In the first speech from this scene Juliet is nervous and anxious to discover what the nurse has accomplished. How could this be shown in her voice? In her movement?

2. How might the nurse's voice reflect her weariness when she returns? What movements would be logical here?

3. Juliet, of course, is impatient to hear the news the nurse brings her. What emotions is she feeling when the woman fails to tell her right away what has happened? How can these emotions be effectively conveyed to an audience?

4. While the nurse is complaining about her physical problems, what actions might she take?

5. After the nurse reveals the plans and tells Juliet to go to Friar Lawrence's cell, the two characters need to react physically to each other since their feelings aren't mentioned in the lines. What could they do?

6. The pace of a play needs to fit the emotional content. Generally, the less serious the content, the faster the pace. Should the pace of this scene be relatively fast or slow? Why?

7. What are the nurse's feelings when she tells Juliet that from now on she should deliver her own messages? How do you think Juliet reacts to this? What voice quality and movements should each use to convey how she feels?

8. What kind of relationship do you think Juliet and the nurse have?

9. Why does the nurse delay telling Juliet about the wedding arrangements?

Blithe Spirit

Noel Coward

C alled an "improbable farce" by its author, this delightfully funny play has many of the characteristics of a drawing room comedy in its treatment of upperclass society. The plot is a variation of the romantic triangle with a humorous twist. The three members of the triangle are Charles, his present wife, Ruth, and his former wife, Elvira, who has been summoned back in spirit form by the spiritualist medium, Madame Arcati. At first Elvira only manifests herself to Charles, but later she moves a vase around the room. Then Ruth also believes in her presence. The problem is that nobody knows how to send her back to the spirit world.

Elvira has a scheme to make Charles a spirit like herself, but there is a slip-up, and Ruth is the one who joins Elvira. Actually, Charles is now happy that both women have gone to the "other side" and he is rid of them. But Charles is not let off so easily. The play ends with things shaking and crashing all through the living room of Charles's house. All the action in the play takes place in this living room. According to Coward, "the room is light, attractive and comfortably furnished."

MADAME ARCATI: Come now—take the plunge—out with it. You've heard strange noises in the night no doubt— boards creaking—doors slamming—subdued moaning in the passages—is that it?

RUTH: No—I'm afraid it isn't.

MADAME ARCATI: No sudden gusts of cold wind, I hope?

RUTH: No, it's worse than that.

MADAME ARCATI: I'm all attention.

RUTH: [*with an effort*]. I know it sounds idiotic but the other night—during the seance—something happened—

MADAME ARCATI: I knew it! Probably a poltergeist, they're enormously cunning, you know, they sometimes lie doggo for days—

RUTH: You know that my husband was married before?

MADAME ARCATI: Yes—I have heard it mentioned.

RUTH: His first wife, Elvira, died comparatively young—

MADAME ARCATI: [*sharply*] Where?

RUTH: Here—in this house—in this very room.

MADAME ARCATI: [*whistling*] Whew! I'm beginning to see daylight!

RUTH: She was convalescing after pneumonia and one evening she started to laugh helplessly at one of the B.B.C. musical programmes and died of a heart attack.

MADAME ARCATI: And she materialized the other evening— after I had gone?

RUTH: Not to me, but to my husband.

MADAME ARCATI: [*rising impulsively*] Capital—capital! Oh, but that's splendid!

RUTH: [*coldly*] From your own professional standpoint I can see that it might be regarded as a major achievement!

MADAME ARCATI: [*delighted*] A triumph, my dear! Nothing more nor less than a triumph!

RUTH: But from my own personal point of view you must see that, to say the least of it, it's embarrassing.

MADAME ARCATI: [*walking about the room*] At last—at last—a genuine materialization!

RUTH: Please sit down again, Madame Arcati.

MADAME ARCATI: How could anyone sit down at a moment like this? It's tremendous! I haven't had such a success since the Sudbury case.

RUTH: [*sharply*] Nevertheless I must insist upon you sitting down and controlling your natural exuberance. I appreciate fully your pride in your achievement but I would like to point out that it has made my position in this house untenable and that I hold you entirely responsible.

MADAME ARCATI: [*contrite*] Forgive me, Mrs. Condomine—I am being abominably selfish—[*She sits down.*] How can I help you?

RUTH: How? By sending her back immediately to where she came from, of course.

MADAME ARCATI: I'm afraid that that is easier said than done.

RUTH: Do you mean to tell me that she is liable to stay here indefinitely?

MADAME ARCATI: It's difficult to say—I fear it depends largely on her.

RUTH: But my dear Madame Arcati—

MADAME ARCATI: Where is she now?

RUTH: My husband has driven her into Folkestone—apparently she was anxious to see an old friend of hers who is staying at the Grand.

MADAME ARCATI: [*producing a notebook*] Forgive this formality, but I shall have to make a report to the Psychical Research people—

RUTH: I would be very much obliged if there were no names mentioned.

MADAME ARCATI: The report will be confidential.

RUTH: This is a small village you know and gossip would be most undesirable.

MADAME ARCATI: I quite understand. You say she is visible only to your husband?

RUTH: Yes.

MADAME ARCATI: "Visible only to husband." Audible too I presume?

RUTH: Extremely audible.

MADAME ARCATI: "Extremely audible." Your husband was devoted to her?

RUTH: [*with slight irritation*] I believe so—

MADAME ARCATI: "Husband devoted."

RUTH: It was apparently a reasonably happy marriage—

MADAME ARCATI: Tut, tut, Mrs. Condomine.

RUTH: I beg your pardon?

MADAME ARCATI: When did she pass over?

RUTH: Seven years ago.

MADAME ARCATI: Aha! That means she must have been on the waiting list.

RUTH: Waiting list?

MADAME ARCATI: Yes, otherwise she would have got beyond the materialization stage by now. She must have marked herself down for a return visit and she'd never have been able to manage it unless there were a strong influence at work.

RUTH: Do you mean that Charles—my husband—wanted her back all that much?

MADAME ARCATI: Possibly, or it might have been her own determination—

RUTH: That sounds much more likely.

MADAME ARCATI: Would you say that she was a woman of strong character?

RUTH: [*with rising annoyance*] I really don't know, Madame Arcati. I never met her. Nor am I particularly interested in how and why she got here. I am solely concerned with the question of how to get her away again as soon as possible.

MADAME ARCATI: I fully sympathize with you, Mrs. Condomine, and I assure you I will do anything in my power to help—but at the moment I fear I cannot offer any great hopes.

Interpretation

1. Madame Arcati is particularly humorous in that she uses everyday language—or at least the language one might expect of a "tweedy," middle-aged Englishwoman—to describe bizarre

and unusual experiences. Are there any other mannerisms of hers that you think make her seem different from other mediums?

2. Why do you think it is an effort for Ruth to tell Madame Arcati what happened? She admits, for instance, that it's embarrassing that Elvira appeared. Why do you think this is so? How would you show this through vocal quality and movement?

3. After a time Madame Arcati begins to repeat what Ruth tells her. Why is she doing this? What are her actions at these times?

4. Madame Arcati is delighted at the news that she is responsible for causing Elvira to materialize. How could you deliver her lines to show this? At the same time Ruth is becoming increasingly more annoyed with the situation and with the medium's reaction to the news. Find specific lines where the annoyance is conveyed. How would you point up these lines?

5. When Ruth says Charles and Elvira had a "reasonably happy marriage," why do you think Madame Arcati replies as she does? For what reason is she chastising Ruth? What actions could she use to communicate her displeasure? What is Ruth's reaction? Why does she pretend to misunderstand?

6. Which of the two characters do you think controls this scene? Point out any specific lines you can find that show this is so.

Act 1, scene 2

The Glass Menagerie

Tennessee Williams

T his play is the story of people trapped by circumstances.
Amanda is trapped by her memories of the past when she
was a southern belle who had many gentlemen callers. Laura,
her daughter, is trapped by her shyness and a physical handi-
cap. Probably as the result of having polio as a child, she wears a
leg brace. Laura's collection of glass animals, from which the
play is named, is very important to her. Her favorite is a unicorn
because, like herself, it is different. Although no age is given for
the characters, we can assume that Laura is in her twenties, and
Amanda probably is in her mid to late forties.

The playwright referred to *The Glass Menagerie* as a memory
play. All the action occurred in the past and is being remembered
by Tom, Laura's brother, who is both the narrator and a
character. The only other character is Jim, who Amanda is
determined will be Laura's "gentleman caller."

First produced in 1944, the play takes place in an apartment in
"one of those vast hive-like conglomerations of cellular living-
units" in an overcrowded city. The apartment faces an alley and
is accessible by a fire escape. Williams is very explicit in
presenting directions for this scene.

Even though the actions are realistic, the play contains a
dreamlike quality, mingling many unrealistic elements with the
realism of dialogue and action. Williams wanted the play presented with all sorts of images projected on a screen. But in the
initial New York production this device was not used, nor has it
often been used since.

In this scene Amanda plays the suffering, domineering mother.
Laura's shyness is revealed by the fact that she quit her typing
class and has been afraid to say so.

SCENE TWO: *"Laura, Haven't You Ever Liked Some Boy?"*

> *On the dark stage the screen is lighted with the image
> of blue roses.*

Gradually, Laura's *figure becomes apparent and the screen goes out.*

The music subsides.

Laura *is seated in the delicate ivory chair at the small clawfoot table.*

She wears a dress of soft violet material for a kimono—her hair tied back from her forehead with a ribbon.

She is washing and polishing her collection of glass. Amanda *appears on the fire-escape steps. At the sound of her ascent,* Laura *catches her breath, thrusts the bowl of ornaments away and seats herself stiffly before the diagram of the typewriter keyboard as though it held her spellbound.*

Something has happened to Amanda. *It is written in her face as she climbs to the landing: a look that is grim and hopeless and a little absurd.*

She has on one of those cheap or imitation velvety-looking cloth coats with imitation fur collar. Her hat is five or six years old, one of those dreadful cloche hats that were worn in the late twenties and she is clasping an enormous black patent-leather pocketbook with nickel clasps and initials. This is her full-dress outfit, the one she usually wears to the D.A.R.

Before entering she looks through the door.

She purses her lips, opens her eyes very wide, rolls them upward and shakes her head.

Then she slowly lets herself in the door. Seeing her mother's expression Laura *touches her lips with a nervous gesture.*

Laura: Hello, Mother, I was—[*She makes a nervous gesture toward the chart on the wall.* Amanda *leans against the shut door and stares at* Laura *with a martyred look.*]

Amanda: Deception? Deception? [*She slowly removes her hat and gloves, continuing the sweet suffering stare. She lets the hat and gloves fall on the floor—a bit of acting.*]

Laura: [*Shakily*] How was the D.A.R. meeting? [Amanda *slowly opens her purse and removes a dainty white handkerchief which she shakes out delicately and delicately touches to her lips and nostrils.*] Didn't you go to the D.A.R. meeting, Mother?

Amanda: [*Faintly, almost inaudibly*]—No—No. [*Then more forcibly*] I did not have the strength—to go to the D.A.R. In fact, I did not have the courage! I wanted to find a hole in the ground and hide myself in it forever! [*She crosses slowly to the wall and removes the diagram of the typewriter keyboard. She holds it in front of her for a second, staring at it sweetly and sorrowfully—then bites her lips and tears it in two pieces.*]

LAURA: [*Faintly*] Why did you that, Mother? [AMANDA *repeats the same procedure with the chart of the Gregg Alphabet*] Why are you—

AMANDA: Why? Why? How old are you, Laura?

LAURA: Mother, you know my age.

AMANDA: I thought that you were an adult; it seems that I was mistaken. [*She crosses slowly to the sofa and sinks down and stares at* LAURA].

LAURA: Please don't stare at me, Mother. [AMANDA *closes her eyes and lowers her head. Count ten.*]

AMANDA: What are we going to do, what is going to become of us, what is the future? [*Count ten.*]

LAURA: Has something happened, Mother? [AMANDA *draws a long breath and takes out the handkerchief again. Dabbing process*] Mother, has—something happened?

AMANDA: I'll be all right in a minute, I'm just bewildered— [*Count five*]—by life. . . .

LAURA: Mother, I wish that you would tell me what's happened!

AMANDA: As you know, I was supposed to be inducted into my office at the D.A.R. this afternoon. [*IMAGE: A SWARM OF TYPEWRITERS*] But I stopped off at Rubicam's Business College to speak to your teachers about your having a cold and ask them what progress they thought you were making down there.

LAURA: Oh. . . .

AMANDA: I went to the typing instructor and introduced myself as your mother. She didn't know who you were. Wingfield, she said. We don't have any such student enrolled at the school!

I assured her she did, that you had been going to classes since early in January.

"I wonder," she said, "if you could be talking about that terribly shy little girl who dropped out of school after only a few days' attendance?"

"No," I said, "Laura, my daughter, has been going to school every day for the past six weeks!"

"Excuse me," she said. She took the attendance book out and there was your name, unmistakably printed, and all the dates you were absent until they decided that you had dropped out of school.

I still said, "No, there must have been some mistake! There must have been some mix-up in the records!"

And she said, "No—I remember her perfectly now. Her hands shook so that she couldn't hit the right keys! The first time we gave a speed-test, she broke down completely—was sick at the stomach and almost had to be carried into the wash-room! After that morning she never showed up any more. We phoned the house but never got any answer"—while I was working at Famous and Barr, I suppose, demonstrating those—Oh!

I felt so weak I could barely keep on my feet!

I had to sit down while they got me a glass of water!

Fifty dollars' tuition, all of our plans—my hopes and ambitions for you—just gone up the spout, just gone up the spout like that.

[LAURA *draws a long breath and gets awkwardly to her feet. She crosses to the victrola and winds it up.*]

What are you doing?

LAURA: Oh! [*She releases the handle and returns to her seat.*]

AMANDA: Laura, where have you been going when you've gone out pretending that you were going to business college?

LAURA: I've just been going out walking.

AMANDA: That's not true.

LAURA: It is. I just went walking.

AMANDA: Walking? Walking? In winter? Deliberately courting pneumonia in that light coat? Where did you walk to, Laura?

LAURA: All sorts of places—mostly in the park.

AMANDA: Even after you'd started catching that cold?

LAURA: It was the lesser of two evils, Mother. [*IMAGE: WINTER SCENE IN PARK*] I couldn't go back up. I—threw up—on the floor!

AMANDA: From half past seven till after five every day you mean to tell me you walked around in the park, because you wanted to make me think that you were still going to Rubicam's Business College?

LAURA: It wasn't as bad as it sounds. I went inside places to get warmed up.

AMANDA: Inside where?

LAURA: I went in the art museum and the bird-houses at the Zoo. I visited the penguins every day! Sometimes I did without lunch and went to the movies. Lately I've been spending most of my afternoons in the Jewel-box, that big glass house where they raise the tropical flowers.

AMANDA: You did all this to deceive me, just for deception? [LAURA *looks down*] Why?

LAURA: Mother, when you're disappointed, you get that awful suffering look on your face, like the picture of Jesus' mother in the museum!

AMANDA: Hush!

LAURA: I couldn't face it.

Interpretation

1. Physical dominance in a play can be shown in a number of ways from having the dominant character upstage to having that person on a higher level. Some other ways are through costuming that calls attention to itself or through movement while the other persons onstage are still. In this scene Amanda is the stronger character. How might you show this dominance?

2. Laura is shy and also handicapped. How might this affect her movement? Her posture? Her gestures?

3. How might Laura's tone of voice change in the line after Amanda asks her her age?

4. Much of what Amanda says to Laura is a put-down. An example is "I thought you were an adult; it seems I was mistaken." Obviously, too, she exaggerates in comments like this. Since this is the case, how might you exaggerate her delivery of this line?

5. Laura at first doesn't know what she's to be accused of. How might she react in showing her puzzlement?

6. Amanda says she's bewildered by Laura's actions. She may or may not be. But as an actress playing Amanda, how could you convince Laura of the truth of the words?

7. Laura probably feels embarrassment, shame, and perhaps fright at her mother's discovery that she has quit the typing class. How might she portray these emotions through voice, movement, facial expression, and gestures?

8. In Amanda's long speech about going to the school, what would be her tone of voice? How could she portray to Laura what she's feeling?

9. How might you express the changes in Laura's feelings in the last two lines of the scene? How might you portray Amanda's reaction?

10. Why do you think Amanda says she became weak and had to be given water when she found out about Laura's quitting school?

11. What can you tell about the relationship between Laura and Amanda from this scene?

Act 2, scene 1

The Lion in Winter

James Goldman

Much more than a typical comedy in its poignancy and exploration of character relationships, this play is the story of the Plantagenets, Henry II of England and his family. Henry and his wife and sons work constantly against one another for power and position.

The scene presented here is between Henry's wife, Eleanor, a crafty, powerful woman whom Henry has had imprisoned, and Alais, Henry's mistress. It is now the Christmas season, and he has had Eleanor released from prison to spend the holidays with her family. Alais is the sister of King Philip of France. She was to marry Henry's eldest son, Richard; instead she has become Henry's mistress. Yet since she grew up around Eleanor, she looks upon her almost as a mother.

The play occurs at Henry's palace in Chinon in the late twelfth century. Rosamund, referred to in the dialogue, was one of Henry's many mistresses.

ALAIS: Did you love Henry—ever?

ELEANOR: Ever? Back before the flood?

ALAIS: As long ago as Rosamund.

ELEANOR: [*Rises, crosses to* C.] Ah, that's pre-history, lamb; there are no written records or survivors.

ALAIS: There are pictures. She was prettier than you.

ELEANOR: Oh, much. Her eyes, in certain light, were violet and all her teeth were even. That's a rare fair feature, even teeth. She smiled to excess but she chewed with real distinction.

ALAIS: And you hate her even now.

ELEANOR: No. . . but I did. He put her in my place, you see, and that was very hard. Like you, she headed Henry's table: that's my chair.

ALAIS: And so you had her poisoned.

ELEANOR: That's a folk tale. [*Crosses to* L. *of bed.*] Oh, I prayed for her to drop and sang a little when she did but even Circe had her limits. No, I never poisoned Rosamund. [*Turns to* ALAIS.] Why aren't you happy? Henry's keeping you. You must be cleverer than I am.

ALAIS: Green becomes you. You must always wear it.

ELEANOR: Are you dressing me in envy?

ALAIS: I've tried feeling pity for you but it keeps on turning into something else.

ELEANOR: Why pity?

ALAIS: You love Henry but you love his kingdom, too. You look at him and you see cities, acreage, coastline, taxes. All I see is Henry. [*Crosses to her.*] Leave him to me, can't you?

ELEANOR: But I left him years ago.

ALAIS: [*Backs away.*] You are untouchable. And I thought I could move you. Were you always like this? Years ago, when I was young and worshipped you, is this what you were like?

ELEANOR: Most likely. [*Sits* L. *end of bed.*] Child, I'm finished and I've come to give him anything he asks for.

ALAIS: Do you know what I should like for Christmas? I should like to see you suffer.

ELEANOR: [*Nodding.*] Alais, just for you.

ALAIS: [*Throwing herself into* ELEANOR'S *arms.*] Maman, oh Maman.

ELEANOR: [*Holding her, rocking her gently, singing softly.*]

The Christmas wine will make you warm—Don't shiver, child.

ALAIS: I'm not.

ELEANOR: The Christmas logs will glow. There's Christmas cheer and comfort here—Is that you crying?

ALAIS: *Non, Maman.*

ELEANOR: Hold close and never let me go.

Interpretation

1. In this scene Alais is trying to dislike Eleanor, whom she really loves. Yet she can't change how she feels since Eleanor has been almost a mother to her. What actions of Alais throughout the scene could show this sense of contradiction?

2. How is Alais feeling when she tells Eleanor she'd like to see her suffer? How could she show this feeling?

3. Eleanor seems to understand and tolerate Alais's feelings for her. How could this understanding be portrayed?

4. The two women obviously care a great deal for each other as can be seen in the last few lines of the scene. How can you physically emphasize these feelings?

5. Eleanor obviously is much more mature than Alais as shown in her indulgent reactions to what the younger woman says. Pick out one or two examples of this indulgence. How would you portray this through facial expression?

6. What should be the predominant mood of this scene?

7. Why do you suppose Alais asks Eleanor if she ever loved Henry?

Act 1

The Importance of Being Earnest

Oscar Wilde

Written in 1895, this play is one of the most enduring of modern comedies. With two-dimensional characters and flippant dialogue, it is an effective satire of upper-class English society. Wilde's use of contrivances of plot and unbelievable situations add to the humor of this polished and highly literate play. Probably the most successful of nineteenth-century comedies, the play pokes fun at Victorian "earnestness" carried to extremes. It, of course, takes place during the Victorian Era of the 1890's.

The plot deals with the problems two young men named Jack and Algernon have in seeking to marry two young women. Cecily loves Algernon, while Gwendolen loves Jack. However, each has said that she could love only a man with the first name of Ernest. So Jack and Algernon have both claimed to be named Ernest. This accounts for the confusion in this scene, which takes place at a country estate.

CECILY: [*Advancing to meet her*] Pray let me introduce myself to you. My name is Cecily Cardew.

GWENDOLEN: Cecily Cardew? [*Moving to her and shaking hands.*] What a very sweet name! Something tells me that we are going to be great friends. I like you already more than I can say. My first impressions of people are never wrong.

CECILY: How nice of you to like me so much after we have known each other such a comparatively short time. Pray sit down.

GWENDOLEN: [*still standing up*] I may call you Cecily, may I not?

CECILY: With pleasure!

GWENDOLEN: And you will always call me Gwendolen, won't you?

CECILY: If you wish.

GWENDOLEN: Then that is all quite settled, is it not?

CECILY: I hope so. [*A pause. They both sit down together.*]

GWENDOLEN: Perhaps this might be a favourable opportunity for my mentioning who I am. My father is Lord Bracknell. You have never heard of papa, I suppose?

CECILY: I don't think so.

GWENDOLEN: Outside the family circle, papa, I am glad to say, is entirely unknown. I think that is quite as it should be. The home seems to me to be the proper sphere for the man. And certainly once a man begins to neglect his domestic duties he becomes painfully effeminate, does he not? And I don't like that. It makes men so very attractive. Cecily, mamma, whose views on education are remarkably strict, has brought me up to be extremely shortsighted; it is part of her system; so do you mind my looking at you through my glasses?

CECILY: Oh! not at all, Gwendolen. I am very fond of being looked at.

GWENDOLEN: [*after examining* CECILY *carefully through a lorgnette*] You are here on a short visit, I suppose.

CECILY: Oh no! I live here.

GWENDOLEN: [*severely*] Really? Your mother, no doubt, or some female relative of advanced years, resides here also?

CECILY: Oh no! I have no mother, nor, in fact, any relations.

GWENDOLEN: Indeed?

CECILY: My dear guardian, with the assistance of Miss Prism, has the arduous task of looking after me.

GWENDOLEN: Your guardian?

CECILY: Yes, I am Mr. Worthing's ward.

GWENDOLEN: Oh! It is strange he never mentioned to me that he had a ward. How secretive of him! He grows more interesting hourly. I am not sure, however, that the news inspires me with feelings of unmixed delight. [*Rising and going to her.*] I am very fond of you, Cecily: I have liked you ever since I met you! But I am bound to state that now that I know that you are Mr. Worthing's ward, I cannot help expressing a wish you were—well, just a little older than you seem to be—and not quite so very alluring in appearance. In fact, if I may speak candidly—

CECILY: Pray do! I think that whenever one has anything unpleasant to say, one should always be quite candid.

GWENDOLEN: Well, to speak with perfect candour, Cecily, I wish that you were fully forty-two, and more than usually plain for your age. Ernest has a strong upright nature. He is the very soul of truth and honour. Disloyalty would be as impossible to him as deception. But even men of the noblest possible moral character are extremely susceptible to the influence of the physical charms of others. Modern, no less than Ancient History, supplies us with many most painful examples of what I refer to. If it were not so, indeed, History would be quite unreadable.

CECILY: I beg your pardon, Gwendolen, did you say Ernest?

GWENDOLEN: Yes.

CECILY: Oh, but it is not Mr. Ernest Worthing who is my guardian. It is his brother—his elder brother.

GWENDOLEN: [*sitting down again*] Ernest never mentioned to me that he had a brother.

CECILY: I am sorry to say they have not been on good terms for a long time.

GWENDOLEN: Ah! that accounts for it. And now that I think of it I have never heard any man mention his brother. The subject seems distasteful to most men. Cecily, you have lifted a load from my mind. I was growing almost anxious. It would have been terrible if any cloud had come across a friendship like ours, would it not? Of course you are quite, quite sure that it is not Mr. Ernest Worthing who is your guardian?

CECILY: Quite sure. [*A pause.*] In fact, I am going to be his.

GWENDOLEN: [*inquiringly*] I beg your pardon?

CECILY: [*rather shy and confidingly*] Dearest Gwendolen, there is no reason why I should make a secret of it to you. Our little country newspaper is sure to chronicle the fact next week. Mr. Ernest Worthing and I are engaged to be married.

GWENDOLEN: [*quite politely, rising*] My darling Cecily, I think there must be some slight error. Mr. Ernest Worthing is engaged to me. The announcement will appear in the *Morning Post* on Saturday at the latest.

CECILY: [*very politely, rising*] I am afraid you must be under some misconception. Ernest proposed to me exactly ten minutes ago. [*Shows diary.*]

GWENDOLEN: [*examines diary through her lorgnette carefully*] It is very curious, for he asked me to be his wife yesterday afternoon at 5:30. If you would care to verify the incident, pray do so. [*Produces diary of her own.*] I never travel without my diary. One should always have something sensational to read in the train. I am so sorry, dear Cecily, if it is any disappointment to you, but I am afraid I have the prior claim.

CECILY: It would distress me more than I can tell you, dear Gwendolen, if it caused you any mental or physical anguish, but I feel bound to point out that since Ernest proposed to you he clearly has changed his mind.

GWENDOLEN: [*Meditatively*] If the poor fellow has been entrapped into any foolish promise I shall consider it my duty to rescue him at once, and with a firm hand.

CECILY: [*thoughtfully and sadly*] Whatever unfortunate entanglement my dear boy may have got into, I will never reproach him with it after we are married.

GWENDOLEN: Do you allude to me, Miss Cardew, as an entanglement? You are presumptuous. On an occasion of this kind it becomes more than a moral duty to speak one's mind. It becomes a pleasure.

CECILY: Do you suggest, Miss Fairfax, that I entrapped Ernest into an engagement? How dare you? This is no time for wearing the shallow mask of manners. When I see a spade I call it a spade.

GWENDOLEN: [*satirically*] I am glad to say that I have never seen a spade. It is obvious that our social spheres have been widely different.

[*Enter* MERRIMAN, *followed by the footman. He carries a salver, table cloth, and plate stand.* CECILY *is about to retort. The presence of the servants exercises a restraining influence, under which both girls chafe.*]

MERRIMAN: Shall I lay tea here as usual, Miss?

CECILY: [*sternly, in a calm voice*] Yes, as usual. [MERRIMAN *begins to clear table and lay cloth. A long pause.* CECILY *and* GWENDOLEN *glare at each other.*]

GWENDOLEN: Are there many interesting walks in the vicinity, Miss Cardew?

CECILY: Oh! yes! a great many. From the top of one of the hills quite close one can see five counties.

GWENDOLEN: Five counties! I don't think I should like that; I hate crowds.

CECILY: [*sweetly*] I suppose that is why you live in town? [GWENDOLEN *bites her lip, and beats her foot nervously with her parasol.*]

GWENDOLEN: [*looking around*] Quite a well-kept garden this is, Miss Cardew.

CECILY: So glad you like it, Miss Fairfax.

GWENDOLEN: I had no idea there were any flowers in the country.

CECILY: Oh, flowers are as common here, Miss Fairfax, as people are in London.

GWENDOLEN: Personally I cannot understand how anybody manages to exist in the country, if anybody who is anybody does. The country always bores me to death.

CECILY: Ah! This is what the newspapers call agricultural depression, is it not? I believe the aristocracy are suffering very much from it just at present. It is almost an epidemic amongst them, I have been told. May I offer you some tea, Miss Fairfax?

GWENDOLEN: [*with elaborate politeness*] Thank you. [*Aside.*] Detestable girl! But I require tea!

CECILY: [*sweetly*] Sugar?

GWENDOLEN: [*superciliously*] No, thank you. Sugar is not fashionable any more. [CECILY *looks angrily at her, takes up the tongs and puts four lumps of sugar into the cup.*]

CECILY: [*severely*] Cake or bread and butter?

GWENDOLEN: [*in a bored manner*] Bread and butter, please. Cake is rarely seen at the best houses nowadays.

CECILY: [*cuts a very large slice of cake and puts it on the tray*] Hand that to Miss Fairfax.

[MERRIMAN *does so, and goes out with footman.* GWENDOLEN *drinks the tea and makes a grimace. Puts down cup at once, reaches out her hand to the bread and butter, looks at it, and finds it is cake. Rises in indignation.*]

GWENDOLEN: You have filled my tea with lumps of sugar, and though I asked most distinctly for bread and butter, you have given me cake. I am known for the gentleness of my disposition, and the extraordinary sweetness of my nature, but I warn you, Miss Cardew, you may go too far.

CECILY: [*rising*] To save my poor, innocent, trusting boy from the machinations of any other girl there are no lengths to which I would not go.

GWENDOLEN: From the moment I saw you I distrusted you. I felt that you were false and deceitful. I am never deceived in such matters. My first impressions of people are invariably right.

CECILY: It seems to me, Miss Fairfax, that I am trespassing on your valuable time. No doubt you have many other calls of a similar character to make in the neighborhood.

Interpretation

1. How do Cecily's and Gwendolen's reactions change toward each other as the scene progresses? How could the changes be reflected in vocal quality, movement, and posture?

2. Pick out as many examples of insults as you can in this scene. How can they be emphasized through body and voice usage?

3. What tone of voice would the two women use in their initial reactions to each other? Why?

4. Much of the humor in comedy comes through exaggeration. Determine as many instances of exaggeration as you can in this scene. How can you point this up for an audience?

5. The two women are caricatures rather than real characters. This means they are both one-dimensional and highly exaggerated. For example, they try to be much more "proper" than is believable. How can you heighten this feeling and make it humorous for an audience?

Scenes for Two Men

The Tragical History of Dr. Faustus

Antigone

Oedipus Rex

Waiting for Godot

The Importance of Being Earnest

scene 5

THE TRAGICAL HISTORY of DR. FAUSTUS

Christopher Marlowe

T his is the story of a man who sells his soul to the devil in exchange for 24 years of infinite knowledge and pleasure. The play, written about 1589, is a tragedy with many comic elements. There are also many instances of magic and supernatural occurrences.

Throughout the play Faustus can save himself by repenting, but he would then have to give up the pleasures provided by the agreement. The conflict in the story is always between repentance and the knowledge and pleasure offered by Satan. At the end Faustus is dragged down to hell.

The following scene occurs in a room in Faustus's house at midnight. Faustus already has agreed to the bargain and merely has to deed over his soul to Satan through Mephistopheles, an angel of hell.

FAUSTUS: Is't not midnight? Come, Mephistopheles!
   Veni, veni,[1] *Mephistophile!*
               [*Enter* MEPHISTOPHELES.]
   Now tell me what says Lucifer, they lord?

MEPHISTOPHELES: That I shall wait on Faustus whilst he lives,
   So he will buy my service with his soul.

FAUSTUS: Already Faustus hath hazarded that for thee.

MEPHISTOPHELES: But, Faustus, thou must bequeath it solemnly
   And write a deed of gift with thine own blood,

[1]come

For that security craves great Lucifer.
If thou deny it, I will back to hell.

FAUSTUS: Stay, Mephistopheles, and tell me, what good
Will my soul do thy lord?

MEPHISTOPHELES: Enlarge his kingdom.

FAUSTUS: Is that the reason why he tempts us thus?

MEPHISTOPHELES: *Solamen miseris socios habuisse doloris.*[2]

FAUSTUS: Why, have you any pain that tortures others?

MEPHISTOPHELES: As great as have the human souls of men.
But tell me, Faustus, shall I have thy soul?
And I will be thy slave, and wait on thee,
And tell thee more than thou hast wit to ask.

FAUSTUS: Ay, Mephistopheles, I give it thee.

MEPHISTOPHELES: Then, Faustus, stab thine arm courageously,
And bind thy soul that at some certain day
Great Lucifer may claim it as his own,
And then be thou as great as Lucifer.

FAUSTUS: Lo, Mephistopheles, for love of thee
[*Stabbing his arm*]
I cut mine arm, and with my proper blood
Assure my soul to be great Lucifer's.
Chief lord and regent of perpetual night,
View here the blood that trickles from mine arm
And let it be propitious for my wish!

MEPHISTOPHELES: But, Faustus, thou must
Write it in manner of a deed of gift.

FAUSTUS: Ay, so I will. [*Writes.*] But Mephistopheles,
My blood congeals and I can write no more.

MEPHISTOPHELES: I'll fetch thee fire to dissolve it straight.
[*Exit.*]

FAUSTUS: What might the staying of my blood portend?
Is it unwilling I should write this bill?
Why streams it not, that I may write afresh?
"Faustus gives to thee his soul"—ah, there it stayed.

[2]misery loves company

Why shouldst thou not? Is not thy soul thine own?
Then write again: "Faustus gives to thee his soul."

[*Re-*]*enter* MEPHISTOPHELES *with a chafer of coals.*

MEPHISTOPHELES: Here's fire; come, Faustus, set it on.

FAUSTUS: So: now the blood begins to clear again;
Now will I make an end immediately. [*Writes.*]

MEPHISTOPHELES: [*Aside*] O what will not I do to obtain
his soul!

FAUSTUS: *Consummatum est-*this bill is ended,
And Faustus hath bequeathed his soul to Lucifer.

Interpretation

1. Faustus probably feels anticipation and excitement at the
thought of getting what he wants by selling his soul. How can
these emotions be portrayed at the beginning of the scene?

2. Mephistopheles can possibly be compared to a salesman
closing a deal. Of course, he's trying to be as persuasive as he
can. How would his voice and movements reflect this?

3. Faustus probably feels a release of tension when he stabs his
arm and realizes that his decision has been made and the deal
completed. How can this be portrayed both vocally and physically?

4. Faustus feels doubt at what he's doing when his blood
congeals. How can this doubt be portrayed?

5. What are Mephistopheles's feelings on his last speech of the
scene? How can these be communicated to an audience?

6. What kind of setting and lighting do you imagine for this
scene?

7. What would be an effective way of staging the scene? How
might you handle Faustus's actions in stabbing his arm?

ANTIGONE

Jean Anouilh

This modern version of a play of the same name written by Sophocles in about 441 B.C. closely follows the original story. Antigone disobeys the orders of her uncle, King Creon, and buries the body of her brother, Polynices, who has rebelled against the king. The king has refused burial because he says the dead man was a traitor. Creon has decreed that anyone caught trying to bury the body will be executed. Now he tells Antigone he'll spare her and kill the guards who found her if she'll agree to tell no one about it and to obey the king's laws in the future. She refuses and is put to death. The king's son, Haemon, who was to marry Antigone, then kills himself.

In this scene, which occurs on the steps of the palace, a guard reports to Creon that against the king's orders someone has attempted to bury the body of Creon's nephew. Although this play takes place in ancient Greece, it usually is done in modern dress.

GUARD: Private Jonas, Second Battalion.

CREON: What are you doing here?

GUARD: It's like this, sir. Soon as it happened, we said: "Got to tell the chief about this before anybody else spills it. He'll want to know right away." So we tossed a coin to see which one would come up and tell you about it. You see, sir, we thought only one man had better come because, after all, you don't want to leave the body without a guard. Right? I mean, there's three of us on duty, guarding the body.

CREON: What's wrong about the body?

GUARD: Sir, I've been seventeen years in the service. Volunteer. Wounded three times. Two mentions. My record's clean. I know my business and I know my place. I carry out orders. Sir, ask any officer in the battalion; they'll tell you. "Leave it to Jonas. Give him an order: he'll carry it out." That's what they'll tell you, sir. Jonas, that's me—that's my name.

CREON: What's the matter with you, man? What are you shaking for?

GUARD: By rights it's the corporal's job, sir. I've been recommended for a corporal but they haven't put it through yet. June, it was supposed to go through.

CREON: [*Interrupts.*] Stop chattering and tell me why you are here. If anything has gone wrong, I'll break all three of you.

GUARD: Nobody can say we didn't keep our eye on that body. We had the two o'clock watch—the tough one. You know how it is, sir. It's nearly the end of the night. Your eyes are like lead. You've got a crick in the back of your neck. There's shadows, and the fog is beginning to roll in. A fine watch they give us! And me, seventeen years in the service. But we was doing our duty all right. On our feet, all of us. Anybody says we were sleeping is a liar. First place, it was too cold. Second place—[CREON *makes a gesture of impatience.*] Yes, sir. Well, I turned round and looked at the body. We wasn't only ten feet away from it, but that's how I am. I was keeping my eye on it. [*Shouts.*] Listen, sir, I was the first man to see it! Me! They'll tell you. I was the one let out that yell!

CREON: What for? What was the matter?

GUARD: Sir, the body! Somebody had been there and buried it. [CREON *comes down a step on the stair. The* GUARD *becomes more frightened.*] It wasn't much, you understand. With us three there, it couldn't have been. Just covered over with a little dirt, that's all. But enough to hide it from the buzzards.

CREON: By God, I'll—! [*He looks intently at the* GUARD.] You are sure that it couldn't have been a dog, scratching up the earth?

GUARD: Not a chance, sir. That's kind of what we hoped it was. But the earth was scattered over the body just like the priests tell you you should do it. Whoever did that job knew what he was doing all right.

CREON: Who could have dared? [*He turns and looks at the* GUARD.] Was there anything to indicate who might have done it?

GUARD: Not a thing, sir. Maybe we heard a footstep—I can't swear to it. Of course we started right in to search, and the corporal found a shovel, a kid's shovel no bigger than that, all rusty and everything. Corporal's got the shovel for you. We thought maybe a kid did it.

CREON: [*To himself.*] A kid! [*He looks away from the* GUARD.] I broke the back of the rebellion; but like a snake, it is coming together again. Polynices' friends, with their gold, blocked by my orders in the banks of Thebes. The leaders of the mob, stinking of garlic and allied to envious princes. And the temple priests, always ready for a bit of fishing in troubled waters. A kid! I can imagine what he is like, their kid: a baby-faced killer, creeping in the night with a toy shovel under his jacket. [*He looks at his* PAGE.] Though why shouldn't they have corrupted a real child? Very touching! Very useful to the party, an innocent child. A martyr. A real white-faced baby of fourteen who will spit with contempt at the guards who kill him. A free gift to their cause: the precious, innocent blood of a child on my hands. [*He turns to the* GUARD.] They must have accomplices in the Guard itself. Look here, you. Who knows about this?

GUARD: Only us three, sir. We flipped a coin, and I came right over.

CREON: Right. Listen, now. You will continue on duty. When the relief squad comes up, you will tell them to return to barracks. You will uncover the body. If another attempt is made to bury it, I shall expect you to make an arrest and bring the person straight to me. And you will keep your mouths shut. Not one word of this to a human soul. You are all guilty of neglect of duty, and you will be punished; but if the rumor spreads through Thebes that the body received burial, you will be shot—all three of you.

GUARD: [*excitedly.*] Sir, we never told anybody, I swear we didn't! Anyhow, I've been up here. Suppose my pals spilled it to the relief; I couldn't have been with them and here too. That wouldn't be my fault if they talked. Sir, I've got two kids. You're my witness, sir, it couldn't have been me as I was here with you. I've got a witness! If anybody talked, it couldn't have been me! I was—

CREON: [*Interrupting.*] Clear out! If the story doesn't get round, you won't be shot. [*The* GUARD *salutes, turns and exits, at the double.* CREON *turns and paces upstage, then comes down to the end of the table.*] A child! [*He looks at* PAGE.] Come along, my lad. Since we can't hope to keep this to ourselves, we shall have to be the first to give out the news. And after that, we shall have to clean up the mess. [PAGE *crosses to side of* CREON. CREON *puts his hand on* PAGE'S *shoulder.*] Would you be willing to die for me? Would you defy the Guard with your little shovel? [PAGE *looks up at* CREON.] Of course you would. You would do it, too. [*A pause.* CREON *looks away from* PAGE *and murmurs.*] A child! [CREON *and* PAGE *go slowly upstage center to top step.* PAGE *draws aside the curtain, through which* CREON *exits with* PAGE *behind him.*]

Interpretation

1. The guard obviously is nervous about having to tell Creon that his orders were not carried out. How might the nervousness be portrayed through voice, gesture, facial expression and/or movement?

2. When Creon threatens to "break" the guards, what emotions is he feeling? How can they be communicated?

3. Creon is angry about what has happened to the body. How could this be reflected in his physical reactions to the guard?

4. How do Creon's feelings change during his last two speeches? How could you portray this to an audience?

5. The stage directions say the guard becomes excited. Why do you think he does? How could this be shown? How might his tone of voice change from the rest of the scene to this last speech?

Oedipus Rex

Sophocles

This play is based on a story in which King Laius of Thebes is told in a prophecy that he will be murdered by his son, who will then marry his own mother. When Oedipus is born, Laius and Jocasta abandon him, but he is raised by another couple. An oracle tells Oedipus the same prophecy, and he flees from the man and woman who have raised him, thinking they are his true parents. While traveling, he has an argument with a man who orders him off the road. Oedipus becomes angry and kills the man who, of course, is his father. Later he is offered the kingship of Thebes and is expected to marry the queen, Jocasta, who is really his mother. All of this is explained at the beginning of the play; none of it is actually a part of the action.

When the play opens, Thebes is experiencing a plague which an oracle says will end when the person who killed Laius is brought to justice. A prophet tells Oedipus he is the murderer, but he refuses to believe him. Jocasta sends for an old shepherd who witnessed Laius's death. He confirms that Oedipus is the murderer. As a result, Jocasta kills herself and Oedipus stabs out his own eyes. He then begs his brother-in-law, Creon, to exile him.

In the following scene the Oracle at Delphi has said that the murderer of Laius must be found and either killed or driven out of the country to end the plague. Oedipus is now consulting with the prophet, Teiresias, to learn the murderer's identity.

OEDIPUS: Teiresias, whose mind can search all things,
    the utterable and the unutterable alike,
    secret of heaven and what lies on earth,
    though you cannot see, you must know how the plague
    afflicts the land.

Our prophet, in you alone we find a protector,
the only savior.
Perhaps you have not been told,
but Phoebus, when consulted, declared
we must discover the slayers of Laius
and slay or drive them out.
Do not, then, spare augury of birds
or any other form of divination you possess
to save yourself and the state,
and to save me and all who are defiled by the deed.
Man's noblest deed is to bring aid by what means he
    has,
and you alone can help.

TEIRESIAS: O fate! How terrible it is to know
    When nothing good can come of knowing.
    I knew of the matter but it slipped out of mind;
    else I would not have come.

OEDIPUS: What now? How can you regret your coming?

TEIRESIAS: Let me go home. You will bear your burden
    easier then,
    and I mine, too.

OEDIPUS: What! You have not spoken loyally or kindly,
    giving no answer with strange words.

TEIRESIAS: Because your own words miss the mark,
    do not expect mine to hit it safely.

OEDIPUS: For the love of God, if you know,
    do not turn away.
    We bend before you; we are your suppliants.

TEIRESIAS: You ask only because you know nothing.
    I will not reveal my grief—I call it mine, not yours.

OEDIPUS: What do you know and refuse to tell?
    You are a traitor if you allow the state to be destroyed.

TEIRESIAS: Since I want no harm for you or myself,
    why do you ask vain questions?
    I will tell you nothing.

OEDIPUS: Worst of traitors,
    you would rouse a stone to wrath!
    Will you never speak out, be stirred by nothing,
    be obstinate to the end?

TEIRESIAS: You see the fault in me but not in yourself.
So it is me you blame?

OEDIPUS: Who would not take offense
hearing you flout the city?

TEIRESIAS: It will come of itself—
the thing that must,
although I breathe no word.

OEDIPUS: Since it must come,
surely you can tell me what it is!

TEIRESIAS: I say no more. Storm at me if you will, you'll hear
no more.

OEDIPUS: And being in such anger, I, for my part,
will hold back nothing, be sure
I'll speak my thought:
Know then I suspect you of having plotted the deed
yourself
and of having done it
short of killing with own hand;
and if you had eyesight,
I would declare the doing too your own.

TEIRESIAS: Was it so?
Well then I charge you to abide by your own decree
and from this day on speak neither to me nor them,
being *yourself* the defiler of the land.

OEDIPUS: So this is your taunt!
And you expect to go scot-free?

TEIRESIAS: I *am* free,
for the truth has made me so.

OEDIPUS: Tell me at least who is in league with you?
For surely this lie was not of your own making!

TEIRESIAS: Yours is the blame,
who spurred me on to speak against my will.

OEDIPUS: Speak again:
Perhaps I did not understand you.

TEIRESIAS: Did you not understand at first hearing?
Or are you bent on provoking me again?

OEDIPUS: No, I did not grasp your meaning.
Speak again!

TEIRESIAS: I say that you are the murderer—
he whom you seek.

OEDIPUS: Now at last, now you have spoken twice,
you shall rue your words.

TEIRESIAS: Shall I speak on
and incense you more?

OEDIPUS: Say what you will; it will be said in vain.

TEIRESIAS: I say, then, you have lived in unsuspected shame
with one who is your nearest,
and you do not yet see the plight you are in.

OEDIPUS: And you expect to go on ranting
without smarting for it?

TEIRESIAS: Yes, certainly, if there is strength in truth.

OEDIPUS: Why, so there is—
except for you; you have no truth,
blind as you are in ears, in mind—and eyes.

TEIRESIAS: Wretched man,
you utter taunts that everyone will soon heap
upon none other than yourself.

OEDIPUS: Night, an endless night is your prison;
you cannot hurt me or any man who can see the sun.

TEIRESIAS: No, it is not your doom to be hurt by me;
Apollo's is the work ahead,
and Apollo's work is enough.

Interpretation

1. What emotions does Oedipus feel when he begins to talk with Teiresias? When and how do these emotions first change? How could you indicate these changes through body movements and tone of voice?

2. Teiresias is fearful of telling who the·murderer is. Yet he is a strong character. How could you play him to show both strength and fear in this scene?

3. Teiresias's feelings change from fear to defiance to anger. Pick out the lines that indicate these changes. How might you show the changes through posture and movement?

4. In a way Teiresias and Oedipus change places emotionally. Oedipus goes from anxiety to anger to fear. What are the specific transition lines from one emotion to another? How could you convey the changes to an audience?

5. This scene starts on a relatively low level of tension and builds. Which lines are transitions between one level of intensity and the next?

6. Which lines provide the high point or emotional climax in this scene? How would you point up these lines and distinguish them from preceding and subsequent lines?

Waiting for Godot

Samuel Beckett

This play is unusual in many ways. Unlike most plays, it has no real progression of action. It merely shows two characters who are waiting for somebody or something to appear, although the audience never learns what. Perhaps Godot represents God, and the waiting shows the hopefulness of humans. On the other hand, Godot never comes. Thus each individual must make his or her own interpretation. Does hope give meaning to life or is it absurd to hope?

The action takes place in the early evening on an endless country road where Estragon and Vladimir are waiting. They complain about life, pretend repentance, and fall asleep. They have nightmares, wake up, and quarrel. They wonder what to expect of Godot if he comes. Much of the action seems to be borrowed from old vaudeville routines. For example, the characters keep putting on and taking off various articles of clothing. In fact, they behave very much like clowns.

After a time, Pozzo, a pompous taskmaster, comes down the road with Lucky. As an ever obedient slave, Lucky has become a near-idiot. Now forced to think, he spouts a mixture of theology and politics before stumbling on down the road with Pozzo. This is the end of Act 1.

During the second act Estragon and Vladimir swap hats, recite what they believe is humorous poetry, play slave and master, and argue about the past, again much as vaudevillians used to do. Pozzo and Lucky come back. Pozzo is now blind and Lucky mute. Neither of them remembers who he is or was. Godot sends a message that he won't come today but certainly will tomorrow. Vladimir and Estragon know they should move on, but neither does. They go on waiting.

VLADIMIR: There's man all over for you, blaming on his boots the faults of his feet. [*He takes off his hat again, peers inside it, feels about inside it, knocks on the crown, blows into it, puts it on again.*] This is getting alarming. [*Silence.* VLADIMIR *deep in thought*, ESTRAGON *pulling at his toes.*] One of the thieves was saved. [*Pause.*] It's a reasonable percentage. [*Pause.*] Gogo.

ESTRAGON: What?

VLADIMIR: Suppose we repented.

ESTRAGON: Repented what?

VLADIMIR: Oh . . . [*He reflects.*] We wouldn't have to go into the details.

ESTRAGON: Our being born?
Vladimir breaks into a hearty laugh which he immediately stifles, his hand pressed to his pubis, his face contorted.

VLADIMIR: One daren't even laugh anymore.

ESTRAGON: Dreadful privation.

VLADIMIR: Merely smile. [*He smiles suddenly from ear to ear, keeps smiling, ceases as suddenly.*] It's not the same thing. Nothing to be done. [*Pause.*] Gogo.

ESTRAGON: [*irritably*] What is it?

VLADIMIR: Did you ever read the Bible?

ESTRAGON: The Bible . . . [*He reflects.*] I must have taken a look at it.

VLADIMIR: Do you remember the Gospels?

ESTRAGON: I remember the maps of the Holy Land. Coloured they were. Very pretty. The Dead Sea was pale blue. The very look of it made me thirsty. That's where we'll go, I used to say, that's where we'll go for our honeymoon. We'll swim. We'll be happy.

VLADIMIR: You should have been a poet.

ESTRAGON: I was. [*Gesture towards his rags.*] Isn't that obvious?

Silence.

VLADIMIR: Where was I? . . . How's your foot?

ESTRAGON: Swelling visibly.

VLADIMIR: Ah yes, the two thieves. Do you remember the story?

ESTRAGON: No.

VLADIMIR: Shall I tell it to you?

ESTRAGON: No.

VLADIMIR: It'll pass the time. [*Pause.*] Two thieves, crucified at the same time as our Saviour. One—

ESTRAGON: Our what?

VLADIMIR: Our Saviour. Two thieves. One is supposed to have been saved and the other . . . [*he searches for the contrary of saved*] . . . damned.

ESTRAGON: Saved from what?

VLADIMIR: Hell.

ESTRAGON: I'm going. [*He does not move.*]

VLADIMIR: And yet . . . [*pause*] . . . how is it—this is not boring you I hope—how is it that of the four Evangelists only one speaks of a thief being saved. The four of them were there—or thereabouts—and only one speaks of a thief being saved. [*Pause.*] Come on, Gogo, return the ball, can't you, once in a way?

ESTRAGON: [*with exaggerated enthusiasm*] I find this really most extraordinarily interesting.

VLADIMIR: One out of four. Of the other three two don't mention any thieves at all and the third says that both of them abused him.

ESTRAGON: Who?

VLADIMIR: What?

ESTRAGON: What's all this about? Abused who?

VLADIMIR: The Saviour.

ESTRAGON: Why?

VLADIMIR: Because he wouldn't save them.

ESTRAGON: From hell?

VLADIMIR: Imbecile! From death.

ESTRAGON: I thought you said hell.

VLADIMIR: From death, from death.

ESTRAGON: Well what of it?

VLADIMIR: Then the two of them must have been damned.

ESTRAGON: And why not?

VLADIMIR: But one of the four says that one of the two was saved.

ESTRAGON: Well? They don't agree and that's all there is to it.

VLADIMIR: But all four were there. And only one speaks of a thief being saved. Why believe him rather than the others?

ESTRAGON: Who believes him?

VLADIMIR: Everybody. It's the only version they know.

ESTRAGON: People are bloody ignorant apes.

Interpretation

1. The mood of this play is one of acceptance and yet hope. Find the lines in the scene that reflect this idea. How can these lines be emphasized?

2. Find lines that show how Estragon and Vladimir feel about each other. How can you portray these emotions?

3. In what ways could you show Estragon's irritability in this scene?

4. How could you show Vladimir's impatience with Estragon?

5. Describe the clothing of Vladimir and Estragon. What are the reasons for your choices?

Act 1

The Importance of Being Earnest

Oscar Wilde

The action occurs in Jack's "luxuriously and artistically furnished" apartment. The place is England of the 1890's. (See p. 47 for further background.) Shortly before the opening of this scene Jack has asked Gwendolen to be his wife, and she has agreed. Then he talked to her mother, Lady Bracknell, about it, and she is concerned about his background. He knows very little about himself. He was discovered in a hand-bag in a railroad station as a baby and, of course, he knows nothing about his family. Lady Bracknell advises him "to try and acquire some relations as soon as possible, and to make a definite effort to produce at any rate one parent, of either sex. . . ."

In the scene that follows Jack is discussing the situation with his close friend, Algernon, who has been in another room and has heard what both Gwendolen and Lady Bracknell have said. The play is a drawing-room comedy, which means first that it is light and witty and second that it deals with the upperclass, of which Jack and Algernon are members. Much of the humor in the play is provided by inverting generally-accepted moral standards. Lady Bracknell, for instance, tells Jack it's good that he smokes because a man needs an occupation.

JACK: Good morning! [ALGERNON, *from the other room, strikes up the Wedding March.* JACK *looks perfectly furious, and goes to the door.*] For goodness' sake don't play that ghastly tune, Algy! How idiotic you are!

[*The music stops and* ALGERNON *enters cheerily.*]

ALGERNON: Didn't it go off all right, old boy? You don't mean to say Gwendolen refused you? I know it is a way she has. She is always refusing people. I think it is most ill-natured of her.

JACK: Oh, Gwendolen is as right as a trivet. As far as she is concerned, we are engaged. Her mother is perfectly unbearable. Never met such a Gorgon. . . . I don't really know what a Gorgon is like, but I am quite sure that Lady Bracknell is one. In any case, she is a monster, without being a myth, which is rather unfair. . . . I beg your pardon, Algy, I suppose I shouldn't talk about your own aunt in that way before you.

ALGERNON: My dear boy, I love hearing my relations abused. It is the only thing that makes me put up with them all. Relations are simply a tedious pack of people, who haven't got the remotest knowledge of how to live, nor the smallest instinct about when to die.

JACK: Oh, that is nonsense!

ALGERNON: It isn't!

JACK: Well, I won't argue about the matter. You always want to argue about things.

ALGERNON: That is exactly what things were originally made for.

JACK: Upon my word, if I thought that, I'd shoot myself. . . . [*A pause.*] You don't think there is any chance of Gwendolen becoming like her mother in about a hundred and fifty years, do you, Algy?

ALGERNON: All women become like their mothers. That is their tragedy. No man does. That's his.

JACK: Is that clever?

ALGERNON: It is perfectly phrased! and quite as true as any observation in civilized life should be.

JACK: I am sick to death of cleverness. Everybody is clever nowadays. You can't go anywhere without meeting clever people. The thing has become an absolute public nuisance. I wish to goodness we had a few fools left.

ALGERNON: We have.

JACK: I should extremely like to meet them. What do they talk about?

ALGERNON: The fools? Oh! about the clever people, of course.

JACK: What fools.

ALGERNON: By the way, did you tell Gwendolen the truth about your being Ernest in town, and Jack in the country?

JACK: [*in a very patronizing manner*] My dear fellow, the truth isn't quite the sort of thing one tells to a nice, sweet, refined girl. What extraordinary ideas you have about the way to behave to a woman!

ALGERNON: The only way to behave to a woman is to make love to her, if she is pretty, and to someone else, if she is plain.

JACK: Oh, that is nonsense.

ALGERNON: What about your brother? What about the profligate Ernest?

JACK: Oh, before the end of the week I shall have got rid of him. I'll say he died in Paris of apoplexy. Lots of people die of apoplexy, quite suddenly, don't they?

ALGERNON: Yes, but it's hereditary, my dear fellow. It's a sort of thing that runs in families. You had much better say a severe chill.

JACK: You are sure a severe chill isn't hereditary, or anything of that kind?

ALGERNON: Of course it isn't!

JACK: Very well, then. My poor brother Ernest is carried off suddenly, in Paris, by a severe chill. That gets rid of him.

ALGERNON: But I thought you said that. . . Miss Cardew was a little too much interested in your poor brother Ernest? Won't she feel his loss a good deal?

JACK: Oh, that is all right. Cecily is not a silly romantic girl, I am glad to say. She has got a capital appetite, goes long walks, and pays no attention at all to her lessons.

ALGERNON: I would rather like to see Cecily.

JACK: I will take very good care you never do. She is excessively pretty, and she is only just eighteen.

ALGERNON: Have you told Gwendolen yet that you have an excessively pretty ward who is only just eighteen?

JACK: Oh! one doesn't blurt these things out to people. Cecily and Gwendolen are perfectly certain to be extremely great friends. I'll bet you anything you like that half an hour after they have met, they will be calling each other sister.

ALGERNON: Women only do that when they have called each other a lot of other things first. Now, my dear boy, if we want to get a good table at Willis's we really must go and dress. Do you know it is nearly seven?

JACK: [*irritably*] Oh! it always is nearly seven.

ALGERNON: Well, I'm hungry.

JACK: I never knew you when you weren't. . . .

ALGERNON: What shall we do after dinner? Go to a theatre?

JACK: Oh, no! I loathe listening.

ALGERNON: Well, let us go to the Club?

JACK: Oh, no! I hate talking.

ALGERNON: Well, we might trot round to the Empire at ten?

JACK: Oh, no! I can't bear looking at things. It is so silly.

ALGERNON: Well, what shall we do?

JACK: Nothing!

ALGERNON: It is awfully hard work doing nothing. However, I don't mind hard work where there is no definite object of any kind.

Interpretation

1. As you saw in the previous scene from *The Importance of Being Earnest* Wilde uses exaggeration to provide humor. Pick out instances of exaggeration in this scene. How can you emphasize this exaggeration for an audience?

2. In what other ways besides exaggeration does Wilde provide the humor in this scene? How can these instances be pointed up?

3. What is the predominant mood of this scene? How can this be reflected in Jack's and Algernon's voices?

4. The beginning exchange and the ending lines give an indication of how Algernon and Jack feel about each other. What can you determine about these feelings? How could you try to make sure they are apparent to an audience?

5. What traits do Jack and Algernon seem to admire in others? Why?

Scenes for
One Man and
One Woman

Oedipus Rex

The Diary of Anne Frank

The Miser

Romeo and Juliet

The Lion in Winter

A Raisin in the Sun

West Side Story

Romeo and Juliet
Photo courtesy of Kent State University
Theatre, Kent, Ohio

Oedipus Rex

Sophocles

Written about 425 B.C., this play was the model upon which Aristotle, the philosopher, based his theories of drama. These theories in turn have influenced the writing of plays ever since. The myth upon which Sophocles based the play was well known to the people of ancient Greece. (See p. 64 for further background.) In fact, earlier playwrights had used it as well. In the version by Sophocles, Oedipus alone is responsible for the tragedy that befalls him. He is the victim of his pride and self-confidence.

As you saw earlier, the play deals with the results of Oedipus's murder of his father, Laius. In this scene Oedipus is beginning to realize that he is responsible for the death of his father and therefore for the plague in Thebes.

JOCASTA: In the name of the gods,
  husband, I beg of you, what was the tale?
  What put you in a rage? Tell me.

OEDIPUS: I will; I honor you more than I honor them:
  Creon has laid a plot against me.

JOCASTA: Husband, be plainer—

OEDIPUS: He declares I am guilty of the blood of Laius.

JOCASTA: So? Did he say he heard it,
  or does he claim to know it himself?

OEDIPUS: Neither: *He* keeps his own mouth unsoiled;
  he made the rogue of a seer his mouthpiece.

JOCASTA: If that is all, prepare yourself to put it out of mind
  at once. Listen to me and learn

that no one born of woman is capable of divination—
as I myself discovered:

To Laius once came an oracle—
I will not say directly from Apollo,
but from his ministers—
that he should die by the hand of a son
born of him and me.
But you must know that Laius, as reported,
was waylaid by robbers
where three highways meet,
and our child, who should have slain him,
if the oracle was true,
was barely three days old when Laius
pinned its ankles together
and had it cast out by servants
on a pathless mountain.
So Apollo did not bring it to pass
that the child should be the slayer of the man
and that Laius should suffer
the thing he dreaded—
death from the hand of the son.
The oracle was clear, yet was proven false, as you see.
So much then for the power of the seers!
What God desires us to know,
be sure he will reveal it himself.

OEDIPUS: Oh wife, wife!
You cannot know what your report has done to me.
What anguish—

JOCASTA: What disturbs you now?

OEDIPUS: I thought I heard you say
Laius was slain where three roads meet—

JOCASTA: Yes, so the report went and so it goes still.

OEDIPUS: And where is this place, Jocasta?

JOCASTA: In Phocis.
Two roads, one from Delphi and one from Daulia, meet.

OEDIPUS: How long ago did all this happen?

JOCASTA: The news was brought to the city
a short time before you became the king.

OEDIPUS: O Zeus! what fate have you stored up for me?

JOCASTA: What is troubling you?

OEDIPUS: No! No questions yet! Tell me only
what sort of man was he? How tall was Laius?
How old?

JOCASTA: He was no longer young—his hair was turning
white,
and he was tall, his figure not unlike your own.

OEDIPUS: I am a miserable man.
An ignorant man, Jocasta, I fear
I have laid myself under my own curse.

JOCASTA: You terrify me, Oedipus. What are you saying?

OEDIPUS: I have a misgiving the seer can see. Just that!
But you can make something plainer. Tell me—

JOCASTA: What? Something makes me tremble,
yet I must answer.

OEDIPUS: Did Laius have few attendants,
or did he travel with a host, as a prince should?

JOCASTA: There were five of them, one a herald;
there was one carriage, for the King.

OEDIPUS: All plain—too plain!
Who told you this, Jocasta?

JOCASTA: The survivor who returned alone. A servant.

OEDIPUS: Is he still in service?

JOCASTA: No longer. When he found you king here on his
return,
in the place of Laius,
he touched my hand and petitioned me
to send him to the fields to pasture flocks.
He asked it as one who found himself ill at ease
in the city and would be far from it.
He deserved more than this consideration,
for, as slaves go, he was a worthy man.
I could not refuse his request.

OEDIPUS: If only we could have him back here quickly!

JOCASTA: He can be brought,
but why do you wish to see him?

OEDIPUS: I fear, Jocasta, I have already said too much.

Interpretation

1. What are the main character traits of Oedipus and Jocasta that are revealed in this scene? How can these be emphasized for an audience?

2. What emotions do you think Oedipus feels when Jocasta tells him of the prophecy and he begins to realize what has happened? How may his tone of voice show this?

3. How do you think the queen reacts emotionally when Oedipus tells her that she cannot know what her report has done to him? What can you do to convey this to an audience?

4. How would you have Oedipus and Jocasta visually react to the increasing tension of the scene?

5. What sort of movement might be effective for the characters? How might this change as the scene progresses?

Act 2, scene 2

THE DIARY OF ANNE FRANK

Frances Goodrich and Albert Hackett

T his play, like *Oedipus Rex,* is a tragedy. But it is entirely
different in scope. Here the heroine is a young Jewish girl
forced to hide from the Nazis. The year is 1944. Anne and her
parents, a sister and four other people are crowded into an
Amsterdam attic where they must remain or be killed. Their only
hope is that Hitler will be defeated, and they will be able to
resume normal lives. Now, however, they think that perhaps the
Nazis are becoming aware of their existence. The play is based
on an actual diary of a young girl who later was killed.

In this scene Anne, now fifteen, is talking to Peter, nineteen,
the first boy she's ever liked and who is one of those who has
shared the attic above the warehouse for two years. This scene
occurs in the bedroom where Peter sleeps. It is one of three
attic rooms into which everyone is crowded. Peter's room is
sparsely furnished with a cot and a chair, and there is barely
room to stand or move around.

ANNE: Look, Peter, the sky. [*She looks up through the
skylight.*] What a lovely, lovely day! Aren't the clouds
beautiful? You know what I do when it seems as if I
couldn't stand being cooped up for one more minute? I
think myself out. I think myself on a walk in the park
where I used to go with Pim. Where the jonquils and the
crocus and the violets grow down the slopes. You know
the most wonderful part about *thinking* yourself out? You
can have it any way you like. You can have roses and
violets and chrysanthemums all blooming at the same

time. . . . It's funny . . . I used to take it all for granted
. . . and now I've gone crazy about everything to do with
nature. Haven't you?

PETER: I've just gone crazy. I think if something doesn't
happen soon . . . if we don't get out of here . . . I can't
stand much more of it!

ANNE: [*softly*] I wish you had a religion, Peter.

PETER: No, thanks! Not me!

ANNE: Oh, I don't mean you have to be Orthodox . . . or
believe in heaven and hell and purgatory and things . . .
I just mean some religion . . . it doesn't matter what.
Just to believe in something! When I think of all that's
out there . . . the trees . . . and flowers . . . and seagulls
. . . when I think of the dearness of you, Peter, . . . and
the goodness of the people we know . . . Mr. Kraler,
Miep, Dirk, the vegetable man, all risking their lives for
us everyday . . . . When I think of these good things, I'm
not afraid any more . . . I find myself, and God, and I
. . . [PETER *interrupts, getting up and walking away.*]

PETER: That's fine! But when I begin to think, I get
mad! Look at us, hiding out for two years. Not able to
move! Caught here like . . . waiting for them to come
and get us . . . and all for what?

ANNE: We're not the only people that've had to suffer.
There've always been people that've had to . . .
sometimes one race . . . sometimes another . . . and
yet . . .

PETER: That doesn't make me feel any better!

ANNE: [*going to him*] I know it's terrible, trying to have any
faith . . . when people are doing such horrible . . . But
you know what I sometimes think? I think the world
may be going through a phase, the way I was with
Mother. It'll pass, maybe not for hundreds of years, but
some day . . . I still believe, in spite of everything, that
people are really good at heart.

PETER: I want to see something now . . . Not a thousand
years from now! [*He goes over, sitting down again on the
cot.*]

ANNE: But, Peter, if you'd only look at it as part of a great
pattern . . . that we're just a little minute in the life . . .

[*She breaks off.*] Listen to us, going at each other like a couple of stupid grownups! Look at the sky now. Isn't it lovely? [*She holds out her hand to him.* PETER *takes it and rises, standing with her at the window looking out, his arms around her.*] Some day, when we're outside again, I'm going to . . . [*She breaks off as she hears the sound of a car, its brakes squealing as it comes to a sudden stop.*]

Interpretation

1. In what ways might it be logical to stage this scene? Where would you place Anne and Peter?

2. What lines best reveal the relationship between Anne and Peter? How can these be portrayed for an audience so they sense the relationship?

3. What is Anne's mood during her first speech? How can it be shown through voice quality?

4. Anne is more accepting of the situation than Peter. How can this contrast be shown in the character's actions?

5. In what manner would you have Peter carry out the action of sitting down on the cot?

6. How would you have each character react to the sound of the car as the scene ends?

Act 2

The Miser

Moliere

This comedy was first performed in Paris in 1669 with the author playing the title role. Moliere, who was credited with introducing literary comedy to France, used a play by the Roman writer Plautus as a starting point for *The Miser*. The play uses stock characters (stereotyped and familiar), slapstick humor, and greatly exaggerated situations.

Harpagon, the miser, has let his greed rule his every action and decision. A widower with two grown children, he is his son's rival, unknowingly, for Marianne's hand in marriage. However, when he has to choose between Marianne and his cash box, he chooses the latter. Harpagon's miserliness is highly exaggerated and is made fun of in many different scenes. In the following scene, he is meeting in his home with the matchmaker, Frosine.

FROSINE: Ah! My, how well you look! You are the very picture of health!

HARPAGON: Who? I?

FROSINE: I've never seen your complexion so fresh and sparkling.

HARPAGON: Really?

FROSINE: Really. You've never in your life looked so young as you do now. I see men of twenty-five who are older than you.

HARPAGON: Nevertheless, Frosine, I'm over sixty.

FROSINE: Well, what is sixty? A mere trifle! It's the flower of one's age, and you are now entering upon the prime of manhood.

HARPAGON: That's true. But twenty years younger wouldn't do me any harm.

FROSINE: You're joking! You don't need them. You're the type that will live to be a hundred.

HARPAGON: Do you think so?

FROSINE: Certainly. You show every sign of it. Hold still a moment! Oh! most certainly, there between your eyes—a sign of long life.

HARPAGON: Do you really know what you're talking about?

FROSINE: Without a doubt. Let me see your hand. My goodness! What a life line!

HARPAGON: Where?

FROSINE: Don't you see how far that line goes?

HARPAGON: Well! But what does it mean?

FROSINE: Upon my word! I said a hundred, but you'll survive one hundred and twenty!

HARPAGON: Is it possible?

FROSINE: They'll have to club you to death, I tell you. You'll bury your children and your children's children.

HARPAGON: So much the better!—But how is our little business going along?

FROSINE: Need you ask? Has anyone ever seen me start anything I didn't finish? I have a marvellous talent, especially for matchmaking. There aren't two people in the world that I couldn't join in a short time. I believe, if I took it into my head, that I could marry the Grand Turk to the Republic of Venice. Of course, there weren't any such great difficulties in your case. As I have business in their house, I have often spoken to both of them about you, and I have told the mother about the future you've been planning for Marianne, since you saw her pass by in the street and take the air at her window.

HARPAGON: What answer did— .

FROSINE: She received the proposition with pleasure. And when I told her you greatly desired that her daughter be present this evening at the signing of the marriage contract here at your house, she consented willingly, and even entrusted her daughter to me for that purpose.

HARPAGON: I have to give a supper for Signor Anselm, Frosine, and I should like her to be present.

FROSINE: You are quite right. After dinner she has to pay your daughter a visit; then she plans to go to the fair, and will return here for supper.

HARPAGON: Very well. They can go together in my coach, which I shall lend them.

FROSINE: That will suit her exactly.

HARPAGON: But, Frosine, have you talked to the mother about the money she can give her daughter? Have you told her that she ought to help a little, if only slightly; that she should make some attempt; that she should bleed herself for an occasion such as this? For, after all, a man does not marry a girl unless she brings along something.

FROSINE: What? This girl will bring you twelve thousand francs a year.

HARPAGON: Twelve thousand francs a year?

FROSINE: Yes. First of all: she has been brought up and nourished on a very sparing diet. She is a girl accustomed to live on salads, milk, cheese, and apples; and, consequently, she does not need elaborate meals, or exquisite broths, or barley syrups all the time, nor all the rest of the delicacies other women need. And they are no slight matter, for year after year they mount up to three thousand francs to least. Besides this, she cares only for what is simple in dress, and does not like gorgeous clothes, expensive jewels, or sumptuous furniture, to which her contemporaries are so much addicted. This saving is worth more than four thousand francs a year. Furthermore, she has a positive loathing for cards, a taste not common in women today. I know of one in our neighborhood who has lost twenty thousand francs at cards this year! But let us figure it at a quarter of that. Five thousand francs a year for cards, four thousand francs for clothes and jewels, make nine thousand francs. And three thousand francs which we set aside for food. Doesn't that make you twelve thousand francs a year all accounted for?

HARPAGON: Yes, that's not bad. But your figures have no reality.

FROSINE: I beg your pardon. Isn't perfect sobriety a real asset in marriage? Or her inheritance of a great love for simplicity in dress? Or the acquisition of a deep well of hatred for gambling?

HARPAGON: It's mockery to make up her dowry with the expenses that she won't run up. I give no receipt for something I don't actually get. I have to put my hands on something.

FROSINE: Great Heavens! you'll put your hands on enough. And they did mention to me some property they own in a foreign country of which you will become the master.

HARPAGON: I'll have to see it. But, Frosine, there is something else that upsets me. The girl is young, as you know, and the young generally like only those of their own age, and seek only their company. I'm afraid that a man of my age won't be to her liking, and that can only produce in my house certain little vexations which wouldn't please me.

FROSINE: Ah! How little you know her! This was one other characteristic that I was going to tell you about. She has a frightful aversion to all young men, and only likes old ones.

HARPAGON: She?

FROSINE: Yes, she. I wish you had heard her on that subject. She cannot bear the sight of a young man. But she says that nothing delights her more than the sight of a handsome old man with a majestic beard. The older they are, the more charming they are for her, and I warn you not to make yourself appear younger than you are. She likes a man to be at least sixty. Not four months ago, on the point of getting married, she promptly broke off the match, when she found out that her lover was only fifty-six and didn't need glasses to sign the marriage contract.

HARPAGON: Just for that?

FROSINE: Yes! She said that she wasn't satisfied with a man of only fifty-six, and, above all, she likes noses with spectacles on them.

HARPAGON: Really, this is something quite new!

FROSINE: It goes even further than I have told you. There are a few pictures and engravings in her room. But what do you think they are? Adonis? Cephalus? Paris? Apollo? Not at all! Fine portraits of Saturn, of King Priam, of old Nestor, and of good father Anchises on his son's shoulders.

HARPAGON: That *is* admirable! I should never have thought it. And my mind is eased to learn she has that attitude. In fact, if I had been a woman, I wouldn't have liked young men either.

FROSINE: I quite believe it. Love young men! What are they but worthless trash! They are mere puppies, show-offs that make you envy their complexions. I'd really like to know who likes them!

HARPAGON: As for me, I don't understand it either. I don't know how some women can like them so much.

FROSINE: One has to be an utter fool to find youth charming! Is that common sense? Are they men, these young fops? Can one really be attached to such animals?

HARPAGON: That's what I say day after day with their effeminate voices, and their three little wisps of beard turned up like cat's whiskers, their straw-colored wigs, their baggy pants, and their fancy waistcoats.

FROSINE: They make a fine comparison next to a man like you. [*To the audience*] Here's a man. There's something here that satisfies the eye. This is the way a man should be made, and dressed, to inspire love.

HARPAGON: You find me attractive?

FROSINE: What? Ah! you are stunning, and your portrait ought to be painted. Turn around a bit, if you please. Nothing could be better. Let me see you walk. [*To the audience.*] Here is a body that is trim, free, and easy in its motions, as it should be, without a trace of any physical weakness.

HARPAGON: Nothing much is the matter with me, thank God. [*He coughs.*] That's only my catarrh, which bothers me occasionally.

FROSINE: That's nothing. Your catarrh is not unbecoming, since you cough with such grace.

HARPAGON: Tell me something. Hasn't Marianne ever seen me yet? Hasn't she ever noticed me in passing?

FROSINE: No, but we have often talked about you. I've sketched a portrait of your person and I've not failed to extol your merits and the advantage it would be to her to have a husband such as you.

HARPAGON: You have done well and I thank you for it.

FROSINE: I have, sir, a small favor to ask of you. There's a lawsuit I am about to lose for want of a little money; and you could easily enable me to win this lawsuit if you would show me some kindness. [HARPAGON *frowns.*] You would not believe how pleased she will be to see you. [HARPAGON *smiles.*] Ah! how you will please her. How admirable an effect on her your old-fashioned ruff will have. But above all, she will be charmed by your breeches, attached to your doublet with laces; that will make her mad for you. And a laced-up lover will be a marvelous treat for her.

HARPAGON: Really! I am delighted to hear you say so.

FROSINE: To tell the truth, sir, this lawsuit is of the greatest consequence to me. I shall be ruined if I lose it. Some slight aid would set right my affairs. [HARPAGON *frowns.*] I wish you could see her rapture when I talk to her of you. [HARPAGON *smiles again.*] Her eyes shone with joy at the recitation of your qualities. In fact, I have made her extremely impatient to see this marriage completed.

HARPAGON: You have given me great pleasure, Frosine, and I assure you, I am deeply indebted to you.

FROSINE: I beg you, sir, to give me the slight help I ask for. [*Harpagon frowns again.*] It will set me back on my feet, and I shall be eternally obligated to you.

HARPAGON: Goodbye! I am going to finish my letters.

FROSINE: I assure you, sir, you could never assist me in a greater need.

HARPAGON: I will give orders for my carriage to be ready to drive you to the fair.

FROSINE: I would not trouble you, if I were not forced by necessity.

HARPAGON: And I'll take care that we dine early so that you won't get sick.

FROSINE: Do not refuse me the favor I beg of you. You would not believe sir, the pleasure that—

HARPAGON: I am going. There! Someone is calling me. Until later. [*Exit.*]

FROSINE: May a fever burn you up! Thieving dog! The devil take you! The skinflint has fended off all my attacks. But I mustn't drop the business now. In any case, there's the other party; I'm sure to be well rewarded there.

Interpretation

1. As is the case with *The Importance of Being Earnest* this play is filled with exaggerated characters and situations. How might you physically exaggerate Harpagon's miserliness in this scene?

2. Frosine flatters Harpagon but really feels contempt for him. How could you physically provide a contrast between these two emotions—one felt and one assumed—to give the audience a glimpse of Frosine's true feelings while keeping them from Harpagon? How could her emotions be exaggerated in her final speech in this scene?

3. Harpagon is a very gullible character, ready to believe whatever Frosine tells him about himself that is pleasant to his ear. How could you, through movement or posture, exaggerate this trait for an audience?

4. Harpagon refers to himself as being over 60. How might you change your voice to portray him?

5. When Frosine speaks to the audience in describing Harpagon, what emotions should she convey? How might this be done?

6. How does Frosine change in manner and speech when asking help with her lawsuit?

7. From what Frosine says, what can you guess about Marianne's home situation?

8. In ways Frosine's motives are obvious. Which lines show this? How can these lines be pointed up for an audience?

9. When Frosine asks for help with the lawsuit, how does Harpagon's reaction to her change? How can this change be effectively conveyed?

Act 2, scene 2

Romeo and Juliet

William Shakespeare

Romeo, who you will recall is a member of the Montague family, attended a masked ball given by the Capulets with whom his family is feuding. There he met Juliet, a member of the Capulet family. Immediately the two young people fell in love. (See p. 29 for further background.)

The scene that follows occurs later that same night when Romeo lingers in the Capulets' garden, under Juliet's window.

[JULIET *appears above at a window.*]
ROMEO: But, soft! What light through yonder window
    breaks?
It is the east, and Juliet is the sun!
Arise, fair sun, and kill the envious moon,[1]
Who is already sick and pale with grief
That thou her maid art far more fair than she.
Be not her maid, since she is envious.
Her vestal[2] livery is but sick and green,
And none but fools do wear it. Cast it off.
It is my lady, oh, it is my love!

Oh, that she knew she were!
She speaks, yet she says nothing. What of that?
Her eye discourses, I will answer it.
I am too bold, tis not to me she speaks.
Two of the fairest stars in all the heaven,
Having some business, do entreat her eyes
To twinkle in their spheres[3] till they return.

[1]the moon goddess, Diana   [2]virgin   [3]transparent shells that carry heavenly bodies around earth

What if her eyes were there, they in her head?
The brightness of her cheek would shame those stars
As daylight doth a lamp; her eyes in heaven
Would through the airy region stream so bright
That birds would sing and think it were not night.
See how she leans her cheek upon her hand!

Oh, that I were a glove upon that hand,
That I might touch that cheek!

JULIET: Aye me!

ROMEO: She speaks.
Oh, speak again, bright angel! For thou art
As glorious to this night, being o'er my head,
As is a wingèd messenger of Heaven
Unto the white-upturned wondering eyes
Of mortals that fall back to gaze on him
When he bestrides the lazy-pacing clouds
And sails upon the bosom of the air.

JULIET: O Romeo, Romeo, wherefore art thou
    Romeo?
Deny thy father and refuse thy name,
Or, if thou wilt not, be but sworn my love
And I'll no longer be a Capulet.

ROMEO: [*Aside.*] Shall I hear more, or shall I speak
    at this?

JULIET: 'Tis but thy name that is my enemy.
Thou art thyself, though not a Montague.
What's Montague? It is nor hand, nor foot,
Nor arm, nor face, nor any other part
Belonging to a man. Oh, be some other name!
What's in a name? That which we call a rose
By any other name would smell as sweet.
So Romeo would, were he not Romeo called,
Retain that dear perfection which he owes[4]
Without that title. Romeo, doff thy name,
And for thy name, which is no part of thee,
Take all myself.

[4]owns

ROMEO: I take thee at thy word.
Call me but love, and I'll be new baptized.
Henceforth I never will be Romeo.

JULIET: What man art thou that, thus bescreened in
night,
So stumblest on my counsel?⁵

ROMEO: By a name
I know not how to tell thee who I am.
My name, dear saint, is hateful to myself
Because it is an enemy to thee.
Had I it written, I would tear the word.

JULIET: My ears have yet not drunk a hundred words
Of thy tongue's uttering, yet I know the sound.
Art thou not Romeo, and a Montague?

ROMEO: Neither, fair saint, if either thee dislike.⁶

JULIET: How camest thou higher, tell me, and wherefore?
The orchard walls are high and hard to climb,
And the place death, considering who thou art,
If any of my kinsmen find thee here.

ROMEO: With love's light wings did I o'erperch⁷
these walls,
For stony limits cannot hold love out.
And what love can do, that dares love attempt,
Therefore thy kinsmen are no let⁸ to me.

JULIET: If they do see thee, they will murder thee.

ROMEO: Alack, there lies more peril in thine eye
than twenty of their swords. Look thou but sweet,
And I am proof⁹ against their enmity.

JULIET: I would not for the world they saw thee here.

ROMEO: I have night's cloak to hide me from their eyes,
And but¹⁰ thou love me, let them find me here.
My life were better ended by their hate
Than death prorogued,¹¹ wanting of thy love.

JULIET: By whose direction found'st thou out this place?

⁵unspoken thoughts ⁶displease ⁷fly over ⁸obstacle ⁹protected
¹⁰if only ¹¹postponed

ROMEO: By love, that first did prompt me to inquire.
He lent me counsel, and I lent him eyes.
I am no pilot, yet wert thou as far
As that vast shore washed with the farthest sea,
I would adventure for such merchandise.

JULIET: Thou know'st the mask of night is on my face,
Else would a maiden blush bepaint my cheek
For that which thou hast heard me speak tonight.
Fain would I dwell on form,[12] fain, fain deny
What I have spoke. But farewell compliment![13]
Dost thou love me? I know thou wilt say "Aye,"
And I will take thy word. Yet if thou swear'st,
Thou mayst prove false. At lovers' perjuries
They say Jove laughs. O gentle Romeo,
If thou dost love, pronounce it faithfully.
Or if thou think'st I am too quickly won,
I'll frown and be perverse and say thee nay,
So thou wilt woo; but else, not for the world.
In truth, fair Montague, I am too fond,[14]
And therefore thou mayst think my 'havior light.
But trust me, gentleman, I'll prove more true
Than those that have more cunning to be strange.[15]
I should have been more strange, I must confess,
But that thou overheard'st ere I was ware,
My true love's passion. Therefore pardon me,
And not impute this yielding to light love,
Which the dark night hath so discovered.

ROMEO: Lady, by yonder blessed moon I swear,
That tips with silver all these fruit-tree tops—

JULIET: Oh, swear not by the moon, th' inconstant moon,
That monthly changes in her circled orb,
Lest that thy love prove likewise variable.

ROMEO: What shall I swear by?

JULIET: Do not swear at all.
Or, if thou wilt, swear by thy gracious self,
Which is the god of my idolatry,
And I'll believe thee.

---

[12]behave according to accepted standards [13]ceremony [14]foolishly affectionate [15]cold in behavior

ROMEO: If my heart's dear love—

JULIET: Well, do not swear. Although I joy in thee,
I have no joy of this contract[16] tonight.
It is too rash, too unadvised, too sudden,
Too like the lightning, which doth cease to be
Ere one can say "It lightens." Sweet, good night!
This bud of love, by summer's ripening breath,
May prove a beauteous flower when next we meet.
Good night, good night! As sweet repose and rest
Come to thy heart as that within my breast!

ROMEO: Oh, wilt thou leave me so unsatisfied?

JULIET: What satisfaction canst thou have tonight?

ROMEO: The exchange of thy love's faithful vow for mine.

JULIET: I gave thee mine before thou didst request it,
And yet I would it were to give again.

ROMEO: Wouldst thou withdraw it? For what purpose, love?

JULIET: But to be frank, and give it thee again.
And yet I wish but for the thing I have.
My bounty is as boundless as the sea,
My love as deep; the more I give to thee,
The more I have, for both are infinite.
I hear some noise within. Dear love, adieu!

    [NURSE *calls within.*[17]]

Anon,[18] good Nurse! Sweet Montague, be true.
Stay but a little, I will come again.   [*Exit.*]

ROMEO: Oh, blessed, blessed night! I am afeard,
Being in night, all this is but a dream,
Too flattering-sweet to be substantial.

    [*Re-enter* JULIET, *above.*]

JULIET: Three words, dear Romeo, and good night indeed.
If that thy bent[19] of love be honorable,
Thy purpose marriage, send me word tomorrow

[16]betrothal [17]offstage [18]very soon [19]intention

By one that I'll procure to come to thee,
Where and what time thou wilt perform the rite,
And all my fortunes at thy foot I'll lay,
And follow thee my lord throughout the world.

Interpretation

1. How would you stage this scene? It probably would help to investigate the public theatres of Elizabethan England to learn how it is believed performances were staged.

2. In Romeo's first speech in the scene he compares Juliet to the sun. What tone of voice would be effective here?

3. What emotions is Juliet feeling during the speech that begins: "O Romeo, Romeo, wherefore art thou Romeo?" How could this be portrayed without making it seem melodramatic?

4. What sort of stance and movement would be effective for each of the performers during the scene?

5. The lines here are very poetic and not at all like people speak to each other—even those newly in love—in everyday life. Yet the scene should be portrayed realistically. How might you phrase the words and lines to assure a realistic tone?

6. There is a fragile quality to the scene. How might you try to maintain it through movement? Voice? Pace?

Act 1, scene 2

THE LION IN WINTER

James Goldman

E leanor and Henry, the king and queen of England in the
late twelfth century, constantly practice intrigues to see who
can outwit the other. Henry has had Eleanor imprisoned because
he recognizes the danger to his rule when she is free. On holidays
he lets her out of the castle where she is held under guard. Despite
this imprisonment, Henry must constantly remain alert to prevent
being outwitted by her. (See p. 44 for further background.)

In this scene the king and queen try to outfox each other once
again. Henry now has so arranged things that his youngest son,
John, will be the next king, while Eleanor has contrived to have
Henry give up his mistress, Alais, sister to King Philip of France.
Alais was reared by Eleanor with the understanding that she
would marry Eleanor's son, Richard. Her dowry consists of a
small country, the Vexin. Henry wants to control the area since
it is strategically located. On the other hand, Eleanor's favorite
son and one who is more in agreement with what she wants is
Richard. If he marries Alais and so gains control of the Vexin, he
thwarts Henry's attempt at gaining more power. John, on the
other hand, is Henry's choice for king because John is such a
simpleton that Henry feels he can control the boy.

HENRY: [*Rises; crosses to* R. *of* ELEANOR] She is lovely, isn't
she?

ELEANOR: Yes, very.

HENRY: If I'd chosen, who could I have picked to love to gall
you more?

ELEANOR: There's no one. [*Moving to the holly boughs.*]
Come on; let's finish Christmassing the place.

HENRY: [*Following her.*] Time hasn't done a thing but wrinkle you.

ELEANOR: It hasn't even done that. I have borne six girls, five boys and thirty-one connubial years of you. How am I possible? [*Picks up three bunches of holly.*]

HENRY: There are moments when I miss you.

ELEANOR: [*Gives* HENRY *two bunches of holly.*] Many?

HENRY: Do you doubt it?

ELEANOR: [*Rumpling his hair.*] That's my woolly sheep dog. [*Crosses* L.] So wee Johnny gets the crown.

HENRY: [*Following her.*] I've heard it rumored but I don't believe it.

ELEANOR: [*Turns to* HENRY] Losing Alais will be hard, for you do love her.

HENRY: It's an old man's last attachment; nothing more. How hard do you find living in your castle?

ELEANOR: [*Placing holly on column* D. S. *of* L. *arch.*] It was difficult in the beginning but that's past. I find I've seen the world enough. I have my maids and menials in my courtyard and I hold my little court. It suits me now. [*Takes bunch of holly from* HENRY *and places on column* U. S. *of* L. *arch.*]

HENRY: I'll never let you loose. You led too many civil wars against me.

ELEANOR: [*Crossing back to* HENRY] And I damn near won the last one. [*Takes last bunch of holly from him and places it on column* U. L. C.] Still, as long as I get trotted out for Christmas Courts and state occasions now and then—for I do like to see you—it's enough. [*Crossing* D. R.] Do you still need the Vexin, Henry?

HENRY: [*Following her.*] Need you ask?

ELEANOR: My strategy is ten years old. [ELEANOR *picks up last bunch of holly and places it on* D. R. *column.*]

HENRY: It is as crucial as it ever was. My troops there are a day away from Paris, just a march of twenty miles. I must keep it.

ELEANOR: [*Surveying the holly.*] I'd say that's all the jollying this room can stand. I'm famished. Let's go in to dinner.

HENRY: [R. C. *Extending his arm.*] Arm in arm.

ELEANOR: [*Taking it, smiling at him.*] And hand in hand. You're still a marvel of a man.

HENRY: And you're my lady. [*She crosses below* HENRY; *they start to exit.*]

ELEANOR: [*Stops.*] Henry, dear, if Alais doesn't marry Richard, I will see you lose the Vexin.

HENRY: Well, I thought you'd never say it.

ELEANOR: I can do it.

HENRY: You can try.

ELEANOR: My Richard is the next king, not your John. I know you, Henry. I know every twist and bend you've got and I'll be waiting round each corner for you.

HENRY: Do you truly care who's king?

ELEANOR: I care because you care so much.

HENRY: I might surprise you. [*Moves* R.; *sits* D.S. *edge of table.*] Eleanor, I've fought and bargained all these years as if the only thing I lived for was what happened after I was dead. I've something else to live for now. I've blundered onto peace.

ELEANOR: On Christmas Eve.

HENRY: Since Louis died, while Philip grew, I've had no France to fight. And in that lull; I've found how good it is to write a law or make a tax more fair or sit in judgment to decide which peasant gets a cow. There is, I tell you, nothing more important in the world. And now the French boy's big enough and I am sick of war.

ELEANOR: Come to your question, Henry; make the plea. What would you have me do? Give out, give up, give in?

HENRY: Give me a little peace.

ELEANOR: A little? Why so modest? How about eternal peace? Now, there's a thought.

HENRY: If you oppose me, I will strike you any way I can.

ELEANOR: Of course you will.

HENRY: [*Extending his arm as before.*] We have a hundred barons we should look the loving couple for.

ELEANOR: [*They stand regally, side by side. Smiling terrible smile at him.*] Can you read love in that?

HENRY: [*Nodding, smiling back.*] And permanent affection.

ELEANOR: [*As they start, grand and stately, for the* L. *arch.*] Henry?

HENRY: Madam?

ELEANOR: Did you ever love me?

HENRY: No.

ELEANOR: Good. That will make this pleasanter.

[*They exit.*]

DIM AND BLACKOUT

Interpretation

1. Trace the changes in emotion in this scene. On what specific lines do changes occur for Henry? For Eleanor? How might changes in voice be used to convey the changes?

2. Should the pace of the scene be relatively fast or slow? Why?

3. Even though Henry and Eleanor are constantly at odds, they have a deep affection for each other. How might this be conveyed?

4. Despite caring for one another, Henry and Eleanor continue their struggle for dominance and power because both are strong people. Both are leaders rather than followers. This need to lead is most important in their lives. In what way can this be conveyed through posture, movement, and facial expression at the end of the scene?

5. Henry and Eleanor have been married for years. Therefore they have great familiarity with one another. They probably know each other's likes and dislikes and one another's idiosyncrasies. How can you show this familiarity in playing this scene?

Act 1, scene 2

A Raisin in the Sun

Lorraine Hansberry

T he action occurs in the Younger family's apartment in
Chicago in the 1950's. It is a neat, clean place although the
furniture has seen better days and the carpeting is wearing
through in spots. The main characters are Mama and her
children, Beneatha and Walter, and her daughter-in-law, Ruth.
Mama is to receive a $10,000 insurance settlement because of her
husband's death. Walter wants to buy a business with it, but
Mama wants to buy a house and also save $3,000 for Beneatha's
education. With great excitement and hope, Mama makes a
down payment on a house. Later, a person from the new neighborhood comes to offer the Youngers money to stay away
because they are black. Walter, who has lost much of the
insurance money, at first wants to accept the money from the
neighborhood group.

The central character in *A Raisin in the Sun* is Walter Younger.
In the play Walter comes to manhood when he sees what truly is
important in life. Mama is a woman who is at peace with herself.
Ruth wants only to help Walter but doesn't know how. Beneatha,
the female in the following scene, is a militant before militancy
was recognized. She is very serious about seeking her roots and
racial identity. Asagai is an African student studying at the
college Beneatha attends.

In the scene that follows Asagai for the first time has come to
Beneatha's apartment, and she doesn't know quite how to react.

ASAGAI: Hello, Alaiyo—

BENEATHA: [*Holding the door and regarding him with pleasure.*]
Hello . . . [*Long pause.*] Well—come in. And please
excuse everything. My mother was very upset about my
letting anyone come here with the place like this.

ASAGAI: [*Coming into the room.*] You look disturbed too . . . Is something wrong?

BENEATHA: [*Still at the door, absently.*] Yes . . . we've all got acute ghettoitus. [*She smiles and comes toward him, finding a cigarette and sitting.*] So—sit down! How was Canada?

ASAGAI: [*A sophisticate.*] Canadian.

BENEATHA: [*Looking at him.*] I'm very glad you are back.

ASAGAI: [*Looking back at her in turn.*] Are you really?

BENEATHA: Yes—very.

ASAGAI: Why—you were quite glad when I went away. What happened?

BENEATHA: You went away.

ASAGAI: Ahhhhhhhh.

BENEATHA: Before—you wanted to be so serious before there was time.

ASAGAI: How much time must there be before one knows what one feels?

BENEATHA: [*Stalling this particular conversation. Her hands pressed together in a deliberately childish gesture.*] What did you bring me?

ASAGAI: [*Handing her the package.*] Open it and see.

BENEATHA: [*Eagerly opening the package and drawing out some records and the colorful robes of a Nigerian woman.*] Oh, Asagai! . . .You got them for me! . . . How beautiful . . . and the records too! [*She lifts out the robes and runs to the mirror with them and holds the drapery up in front of herself.*]

ASAGAI: [*Coming to her at the mirror.*] I shall have to teach you how to drape it properly. [*He flings the material about her for the moment and stands back to look at her.*] Ah—Oh-pay-gay-day, oh-gbah-mu-shay. [*A Yoruba exclamation for admiration.*] You wear it well . . . very well . . . mutilated hair and all.

BENEATHA: [*Turning suddenly.*] My hair—what's wrong with my hair?

ASAGAI: [*Shrugging.*] Were you born with it like that?

BENEATHA: [*Reaching up to touch it.*] No . . . of course not. [*She looks back to the mirror, disturbed.*]

ASAGAI: [*Smiling.*] How then?

BENEATHA: You know perfectly well how . . . as crinkly as yours . . . that's how.

ASAGAI: And it is ugly to you that way?

BENEATHA: [*Quickly.*] Oh, no—not ugly . . . [*More slowly, apologetically.*] But it's so hard to manage when it's, well —raw.

ASAGAI: And so to accommodate that—you mutilated it every week?

BENEATHA: It's not mutilation!

ASAGAI: [*Laughing aloud at her seriousness.*] Oh . . . please! I am only teasing you because you are so very serious about these things. [*He stands back from her and folds his arms across his chest as he watches her pulling at her hair and frowning in the mirror.*] Do you remember the first time you met me at school? . . . [*He laughs.*] You came up to me and you said—and I thought you were the most serious little thing I had ever seen—you said: [*He imitates her.*] "Mr. Asagai—I want very much to talk with you. About Africa. You see, Mr. Asagai, I am looking for my identity!" [*He laughs.*]

BENEATHA: [*Turning to him, not laughing.*] Yes—[*Her face is quizzical, profoundly disturbed.*]

ASAGAI: [*Still teasing and reaching out and taking her face in his hands and turning her profile to him.*] Well . . . it is true that this is not so much a profile of a Hollywood queen as perhaps a queen of the Nile—[*A mock dismissal of the importance of the question.*] But what does it matter? Assimilationism is so popular in your country.

BENEATHA: [*Wheeling, passionately, sharply.*] I am not an assimilationist!

ASAGAI: [*The protest hangs in the room for a moment and* ASAGAI *studies her, his laughter fading.*] Such a serious one. [*There is a pause.*] So—you like the robes? You must take excellent care of them—they are from my sister's personal wardrobe.

BENEATHA: [*With incredulity.*] You—you sent all the way home—for me?

ASAGAI: [*With charm.*] For you—I would do much more . . . Well, that is what I came for. I must go.

BENEATHA: Will you call me Monday?

ASAGAI: Yes . . . We have a great deal to talk about. I mean about identity and time and all that.

BENEATHA: Time?

ASAGAI: Yes. About how much time one needs to know what one feels.

BENEATHA: You never understood that there is more than one kind of feeling which can exist between a man and a woman—or, at least, there should be.

ASAGAI: [*Shaking his head negatively but gently.*] No. Between a man and a woman there need be only one kind of feeling. I have that for you . . . Now even . . . right this moment . . .

BENEATHA: I know—and by itself—it won't do. I can find that anywhere.

ASAGAI: For a woman it should be enough.

BENEATHA: I know—because that's what it says in all the novels that men write. But it isn't. Go ahead and laugh —but I'm not interested in being someone's little episode in America or—[*With feminine vengeance.*]—one of them! [ASAGAI *has burst into laughter again.*] That's funny as hell, huh!

ASAGAI: It's just that every American girl I have known has said that to me. White—black—in this you are all the same. And the same speech, too!

BENEATHA: [*Angrily.*] Yuk, yuk, yuk!

ASAGAI: It's how you can be sure that the world's most liberated women are not liberated at all. You all talk about it too much!

Interpretation

1. The stage directions in this scene say that Beneatha is to appear childlike when she asks Asagai what he brought her. How might she do this?

2. In this scene Beneatha tries to appear different than she really is. In what ways does she do this? How can this idea be pointed up through use of the voice?

3. Asagai's feelings for Beneatha are much more real than her feelings for him. How can you bring out this idea through the use of the voice?

4. How does Asagai feel about Beneatha's seriousness? He laughs at it, but why? How can you try to assure that the audience will understand his emotions?

5. The stage directions say that Beneatha is incredulous that Asagai sent for his sister's robes for her. Why do you think this is so? What else does she feel? How can you convey these feelings to an audience?

6. What are Beneatha's feelings at the end of the scene when Asagai says she's not liberated? How can you communicate these feelings to the audience?

7. Why is Beneatha so much against "assimilation?"

8. Why do you think Asagai teases Beneatha about her hair?

Act 1, scene 7

WEST SIDE STORY

Arthur Laurents, Leonard Bernstein, Stephen Sondheim

The original idea for *West Side Story* came from the choreographer, Jerome Robbins. Arthur Laurents wrote the script, Leonard Bernstein composed the music, and Stephen Sondheim write the lyrics. Based on Shakespeare's *Romeo and Juliet,* with its feuding families, *West Side Story* portrays a different kind of feud. It's between the Sharks, a Puerto Rican street gang, and the Jets, another New York gang made up of Americans. It is the love story of Tony, an American, and Maria, a Puerto Rican, but it also deals with the problems of prejudice and teenage gang rivalry.

The following scene occurs the day after Tony and Maria have met and fallen in love. Despite being associated with others on opposite sides of the feud, they make plans to marry. Maria's brother, Bernardo, is the leader of the Sharks; Anita is his girlfriend. Tony is the former leader of the Jets. Shortly before the opening of this scene, Anita has said she won't tell anyone that Tony has come to see Maria. She is the person Tony refers to in the opening line. The action takes place in a bridal shop where Maria works.

TONY: Don't worry. She likes us!

MARIA: But she is worried.

TONY: She's foolish. We're untouchable; we *are* in the air; we have magic!

MARIA: Magic is also evil and black. Are you going to that rumble?

TONY: No.

MARIA: Yes.

TONY: Why??

MARIA: You must go and stop it.

TONY: I have stopped it! It's only a fist fight. 'Nardo won't get—

MARIA: *Any* fight is not good for us.

TONY: Everything is good for us and we are good for everything.

MARIA: Listen and *hear* me. You must go and stop it.

TONY: Then I will.

MARIA: [*surprised*] Can you?

TONY: You don't want even a fist fight? There won't be any fight.

MARIA: I believe you! You *do* have magic.

TONY: Of course, I have you. You go home and dress up. Then tonight, I will come by for you.

MARIA: You cannot come by. My mama . . .

TONY: [*after a pause*] Then I will take you to my house—

MARIA: [*shaking her head*] *Your* mama . . .

[*Another awkward pause. Then he sees a female dummy and pushes it forward.*]

TONY: She will come running from the kitchen to welcome you. She lives in the kitchen.

MARIA: Dressed so elegant?

TONY: I told her you were coming. She will look at your face and try not to smile. And she will say: Skinny—but pretty.

MARIA: She is plump, no doubt.

TONY: [*holding out the waist of the dummy's dress*] Fat!

MARIA: [*indicating another female dummy*] I take after my mama; delicate-boned. [*He kisses her.*] Not in front of Mama! [*He turns the dummy around as she goes to a male dummy.*] Oh, I would like to see Papa in this!

Mama will make him ask about your prospects, if you go to church. But Papa—Papa *might* like you.

TONY: [*kneeling to the "father" dummy*] May I have your daughter's hand?

MARIA: He says yes.

TONY: *Gracias!*

MARIA: And your mama?

TONY: I'm afraid to ask her.

MARIA: Tell her she's not getting a daughter; she's getting rid of a son!

TONY: She says yes.

MARIA: She has good taste. [*She grabs up the wedding veil and puts it on as* TONY *arranges the dummies.*]

TONY: Maid of honor!

MARIA: That color is bad for Anita.

TONY: Best man!

MARIA: That is my Papa!

TONY: Sorry, Papa. Here we go, Riff: Womb to Tomb! [*He takes hat off dummy.*]

MARIA: Now you see, Anita, I told you there was nothing to worry about.

[*Music starts as she leaves the dummy and walks up to* TONY. *They look at each other—and the play acting vanishes. Slowly, seriously, they turn front, and together kneel as before an altar.*]

TONY: I, Anton, take thee, Maria . . .

MARIA: I, Maria, take thee, Anton . . .

TONY: For richer, for poorer . . .

MARIA: In sickness and in health . . .

TONY: To love and to honor . . .

MARIA: To hold and to keep . . .

TONY: From each sun to each moon . . .

MARIA: From tomorrow to tomorrow . . .

TONY: From now to forever . . .

MARIA: Till death do us part.

TONY: With this ring, I thee wed.

MARIA: With this ring, I thee wed.

TONY: [*sings*] Make of our hands one hand,
Make of our hearts one heart,
Make of our vows one last vow:
Only death will part us now.

MARIA: Make of our lives one life,
Day after day, one life.

BOTH: Now it begins, now we start
One hand, one heart——
Even death won't part us now.

[*They look at each other, then at the reality of their "game."
They smile tenderly, ruefully, and slowly put the dummies
back into position. Though brought back to earth, they
continue to sing.*]

Make of our lives one life,
Day after day, one life.
Now it begins, now we start
One hand, one heart—
Even death won't part us now.

[*Very gently, he kisses her hand.*]

The Lights Fade Out.

Interpretation

1. Tony and Maria have great tenderness for one another. What
might they do to express this through movement or facial
expression?

2. On what line do Tony and Maria begin "play acting?" What
could you do vocally as well as physically to show the contrast
between this portion of the scene and what has preceded it?

3. Despite the fact that Tony and Maria are "acting" through the
second part of the scene, they obviously are presenting true

feelings. What are these feelings? How can they be presented to an audience?

4. At one point in the scene the stage directions indicate that the "play acting" between Tony and Maria is to end. What does this mean? How have they been play acting? They are still pretending as they kneel before a make-believe altar. How does this differ from the way they had been acting? How can you make this difference readily apparent to an audience?

5. The last part of the scene is much more serious in nature than the rest. How can you immediately set this tone of seriousness for the audience?

6. What do you think makes *West Side Story* such an enduring and popular play?

7. Would you like to play one of the leads in a full production of this musical? Why or why not?

Scenes for Three Persons

A Raisin in the Sun

Macbeth

An Enemy of the People

Blithe Spirit

No Exit

A Raisin in the Sun
Photo by Bill Reid
Courtesy of the Old Globe Theatre,
San Diego, California

Act 1, scene 1

A Raisin in the Sun

Lorraine Hansberry

You have already learned that the playwright wanted to present three types of women in her play. This scene clearly shows the different attitudes toward life of the three women. Mama is pretty much set in her ways and embraces the more traditional values of right and wrong. Ruth tends to agree with Mama but isn't as much at ease with herself as Mama. In fact, she's uncertain about many things. Beneatha is the militant, ready to embrace the new in opposition to the old. At the same time she flits from one set of interests to another. She has taken to heart the idea that a person must discover her identity. She doesn't realize how foolish her unshakeable and absolute beliefs are to others. She is absorbed in herself and so defiantly flaunts attitudes that go against what others in her family believe. (See p. 106 for further background.)

Just before the scene opens Beneatha has used profanity about an upstairs neighbor's use of a vacuum cleaner.

MAMA: If you use the Lord's name just one more time—

BENEATHA: [*A bit of a whine.*] Oh, Mama—

RUTH: Fresh—just fresh as salt, this girl!

BENEATHA: [*Drily.*] Well—if the salt loses its savor—

MAMA: Now that will do. I just ain't going to have you 'round here reciting the scriptures in vain—you hear me?

BENEATHA: How did I manage to get on everybody's wrong side by just walking into a room?

RUTH: If you weren't so fresh—

BENEATHA: Ruth, I'm twenty years old.

MAMA: What time you be home from school today?

BENEATHA: Kind of late. [*With enthusiasm.*] Madeline is going to start my guitar lessons today.

[MAMA *and* RUTH *look up with the same expression.*]

MAMA: Your *what* kind of lessons?

BENEATHA: Guitar.

RUTH: Oh, Father!

MAMA: How come you done taken it in your mind to learn to play the guitar?

BENEATHA: I just want to, that's all.

MAMA: [*Smiling.*] Lord, child, don't you know what to do with yourself? How long is it going to be before you get tired of this now—like you got tired of that little play-acting group you joined last year? [*Looking at* RUTH.] And what was it the year before that?

RUTH: The horseback-riding club for which she bought that fifty-five-dollar riding habit that's been hanging in the closet ever since!

MAMA: [*To* BENEATHA] Why you got to flit so from one thing to another, baby?

BENEATHA: [*Sharply.*] I just want to learn to play the guitar. Is there anything wrong with that?

MAMA: Ain't nobody trying to stop you. I just wonders sometimes why you has to flit so from one thing to another all the time. You ain't never done nothing with all that camera equipment you brought home—

BENEATHA: I don't flit! I—I experiment with different forms of expression—

RUTH: Like riding a horse?

BENEATHA: People have to express themselves one way or another.

MAMA: What is it you want to express?

BENEATHA: [*Angrily.*] Me! [MAMA *and* RUTH *look at each other and burst into raucous laughter.*] Don't worry—I don't expect you to understand.

MAMA: [*To change the subject.*] Who are you going out with tomorrow night?

BENEATHA: [*With displeasure.*] George Murchison again.

MAMA: [*Pleased.*] Oh—you getting a little sweet on him?

RUTH: You ask me, this child ain't sweet on nobody but herself—[*Underbreath.*] Express herself! [*They laugh.*]

BENEATHA: Oh—I like George all right, Mama. I mean I like him enough to go out with him and stuff, but—

RUTH: [*For devilment.*] What does *and stuff* mean?

BENEATHA: Mind your own business.

MAMA: Stop picking at her now, Ruth. [*A thoughtful pause, and then a suspicious sudden look at her daughter as she turns in her chair for emphasis.*] What *does* it mean?

BENEATHA: [*Wearily.*] Oh, I just mean I couldn't ever really be serious about George. He's—he's so shallow.

RUTH: Shallow—what do you mean he's shallow? He's *Rich!*

MAMA: Hush, Ruth.

BENEATHA: I know he's rich. He knows he's rich, too.

RUTH: Well—what other qualities a man got to have to satisfy you, little girl?

BENEATHA: You wouldn't even begin to understand. Anybody who married Walter could not possibly understand.

MAMA: [*Outraged.*] What kind of way is that to talk about your brother?

BENEATHA: Brother is a flip—let's face it.

MAMA: [*To* RUTH, *helplessly.*] What's a flip?

RUTH: [*Glad to add kindling.*] She's saying he's crazy.

BENEATHA: Not crazy. Brother isn't really crazy yet—he—he's an elaborate neurotic.

MAMA: Hush your mouth!

BENEATHA: As for George. Well. George looks good—he's got a beautiful car and he takes me to nice places and, as my sister-in-law says, he is probably the richest boy I will ever get to know and I even like him sometimes—but if the Youngers are sitting around waiting to see if their little Bennie is going to tie up the family with the Murchisons, they are wasting their time.

RUTH: You mean you wouldn't marry George Murchison if he asked you someday? That pretty, rich thing? Honey, I knew you was odd—

BENEATHA: No I would not marry him if all I felt for him was what I feel for him now. Besides, George's family wouldn't really like it.

MAMA: Why not?

BENEATHA: Oh, Mama—The Murchisons are honest-to-God-real-*live* rich colored people, and the only people in the world who are more snobbish than rich white people are rich colored people. I thought everybody knew that. I've met Mrs. Murchison. She's a scene!

MAMA: You must not dislike people 'cause they well off, honey.

BENEATHA: Why not? It makes just as much sense as disliking people 'cause they are poor, and lots of people do that.

RUTH: [*A wisdom-of-the-ages manner. To* MAMA.] Well, she'll get over some of this—

BENEATHA: Get over it? What are you talking about, Ruth? Listen, I'm going to be a doctor. I'm not worried about who I'm going to marry yet—if I ever get married.

MAMA *and* RUTH: *If*!

MAMA: Now, Bennie—

BENEATHA: Oh, I probably will . . . but first I'm going to be a doctor, and George, for one, still thinks that's pretty funny. I couldn't be bothered with that. I am going to be a doctor and everybody around here better understand that!

MAMA: [*Kindly.*] 'Course you going to be a doctor, honey, God willing.

BENEATHA: [*Drily.*] God hasn't got a thing to do with it.

MAMA: Beneatha—that just wasn't necessary.

BENEATHA: Well—neither is God. I get sick of hearing about God.

MAMA: Beneatha!

BENEATHA: I mean it! I'm just tired of hearing about God all the time. What has He got to do with anything? Does he pay tuition?

MAMA: You 'bout to get your fresh little jaw slapped!

RUTH: That's just what she needs, all right!

BENEATHA: Why? Why can't I say what I want to around here, like everybody else?

MAMA: It don't sound nice for a young girl to say things like that —you wasn't brought up that way. Me and your father went to trouble to get you and Brother to church every Sunday.

BENEATHA: Mama, you don't understand. It's all a matter of ideas, and God is just one idea I don't accept. It's not important. I am not going out and be immoral or commit crimes because I don't believe in God. I don't even think about it. It's just that I get tired of Him getting credit for all the things the human race achieves through its own stubborn effort. There simply is no blasted God—there is only man and it is he who makes miracles!

[MAMA absorbs this speech, studies her daughter and rises slowly and crosses to BENEATHA and slaps her powerfully across the face. After, there is only silence and the daughter drops her eyes from her mother's face, and MAMA is very tall before her.]

MAMA: Now—you say after me, in my mother's house there is still God. [There is a long pause and BENEATHA stares at the floor wordlessly. MAMA repeats the phrase with precision and cool emotion.] In my mother's house there is still God.

BENEATHA: In my mother's house there is still God.

[A long pause.]

MAMA: [Walking away from BENEATHA, too disturbed for triumphant posture. Stopping and turning back to her daughter.] There are some ideas we ain't going to have in this house. Not long as I am at the head of this family.

BENEATHA: Yes, ma'am.

[MAMA *walks out of the room.*]

Interpretation

1. Mama and Beneatha both are strong characters. At different points in the scene one or the other is dominant. Which lines that show the most strength and dominance? How can these be emphasized vocally?

2. Dominance has a lot to do with placement on the stage. How would you place the three characters at the beginning of the scene? How and where might the placement change throughout?

3. Ruth is feeling disappointed with Beneatha throughout the scene. How could you present this idea so the audience immediately grasps what she feels?

4. How do Mama and Ruth react to Beneatha's announcement that she's starting guitar lessons? What changes in their voices could reflect their reactions?

5. For most of the scene Ruth and Mama represent one point of view and Beneatha another. How can you emphasize this through placement and movement?

6. Beneatha is exasperated by being accused of flitting from one thing to another. How can you show this through voice usage and quality?

7. Ruth is shocked when Beneatha says George is shallow. Why? How can you point up this idea vocally?

8. Why are Mama and Ruth shocked when Beneatha implies that she won't marry? How can this shock be physically emphasized? What could be Beneatha's reaction to the other two?

9. In what ways in this scene is Beneatha's immaturity revealed?

10. What causes the tension in this scene? On what lines does it intensify?

Act 4, scene 1

Macbeth

William Shakespeare

T he title character in this play has been proclaimed king
after secretly murdering the ruling monarch, Duncan of
Scotland. Three witches had foretold that Macbeth would become
king. Now he is seen as a blood-thirsty tyrant who will stop at
nothing to achieve his ends. Others are now plotting against
him. He therefore goes to the witches' cavern once more to have
them prophesy what his fate will be. This scene occurs just before
his arrival there.

A cavern. In the middle, a boiling caldron.
[*Thunder. Enter the* THREE WITCHES.]

FIRST WITCH: Thrice the brinded[1] cat hath mewed.

SECOND WITCH: Thrice and once the hedgepig[2] whined.

THIRD WITCH: Harpier[3] cries "'Tis time, 'tis time."

FIRST WITCH: Round about the caldron go.
In the poisoned entrails throw.
Toad, that under cold stone
Days and nights has thirty-one
Sweltered venom[4] sleeping got,
Boil thou first i' the charmed pot.

ALL: Double, double toil and trouble,
Fire burn and caldron bubble.

SECOND WITCH: Fillet of a fenny[5] snake,
In the caldron boil and bake.

[1]striped [2]hedgehog [3]familiar spirit [4]sweated out poison of
the toad [5]from a swamp

Eye of newt and toe of frog,
Wool of bat and tongue of dog,
Adder's fork[6] and blindworm's[7] sting,
Lizard's leg and howlet's[8] wing,
For a charm of powerful trouble,
Like a Hell broth boil and bubble.

ALL: Double, double toil and trouble,
Fire burn and caldron bubble.

THIRD WITCH: Scale of dragon, tooth of wolf,
Witches' mummy,[9] maw and gulf[10]
Of the ravined[11] salt-sea shark,
Root of hemlock digged i'the dark,
Liver of blaspheming Jew,
Gall of goat and slips of yew
Slivered[12] in the moon's eclipse,
Nose of Turk and Tartar's lips,
Finger of birth-strangled babe
Ditch-delivered[13] by a drab,
Make the gruel thick and slab.[14]
Add thereto a tiger's chaudron,[15]
For the ingredients of our caldron.

ALL: Double, double toil and trouble,
Fire burn and caldron bubble.

SECOND WITCH: Cool it with a baboon's blood,
Then the charm is firm and good.

Interpretation

1. How might you want to stage this scene? Why?

2. What mood would you want to create for the scene? Why?
How could you do this through movement and voice?

3. What would you want to convey through facial expression in
the scene? Why? How would you do it?

[6]forked tongue [7]a small, harmless lizard without legs [8]small
owl [9]mummy from Egypt was considered a powerful drug [10]belly
and gullet [11]ravenous [12]sliced [13]born in a ditch [14]like thick
mud [15]entrails

4. None of the three witches in this scene is dominant or stronger than the other. How can you ensure that the witches are correctly played?

5. What sort of pace should the scene have? Why?

6. How can you effectively use voice and movement to make each witch an individual?

7. What are the most important ideas in this scene? How can you emphasize these ideas for an audience?

Act 1

An Enemy
of the People

Henrik Ibsen

This play written by Ibsen, a Norwegian playwright, in 1882, concerns Dr. Stockmann, a scientist who has discovered that the town's water is being polluted by wastes from his father-in-law's tannery. When he makes the findings public, the town turns against him because public baths provide much of the town's livelihood. If word gets out that the baths, which are intended as a health resort, are contaminated, many people will lose their incomes. Nevertheless, Stockmann stands up for what he believes.

In the scene that follows Hovstad and Alaksen, a newspaper editor and a printer, have heard that Stockmann's father-in-law is buying up stock in the baths, apparently looking to make a profit. They believe that once the father-in-law has all the stock, Dr. Stockmann will then declare the baths free of contamination. Since they assume that Dr. Stockmann is in on a deal to make a lot of money, they want a cut of the profits. Stockmann is innocent of any such scheme. Meant to take place in the time Ibsen wrote it, the play is now staged as a period piece. This scene occurs in Stockmann's house.

DR. STOCKMANN: Well, what do you want with me? Be brief.

HOVSTAD: I can quite understand that you resent our attitude at the meeting yesterday—

DR. STOCKMANN: Your attitude, you say? Yes, it was a pretty attitude! I call it the attitude of cowards—of old women— Shame upon you!

HOVSTAD: Call it what you will; but we could not act otherwise.

DR. STOCKMANN: You dared not, I suppose? Isn't that so?

HOVSTAD: Yes, if you like to put it so.

ASLAKSEN: But why didn't you just say a word to us beforehand? The merest hint to Mr. Hovstad or to me—

DR. STOCKMANN: A hint? What about?

ASLAKSEN: About what was really behind it all.

DR. STOCKMANN: I don't in the least understand you?

ASLAKSEN: [*Nods confidentially.*] Oh yes, you do, Dr. Stockmann.

HOVSTAD: It's no good making a mystery of it any longer.

DR. STOCKMANN: [*Looking from one to the other.*] Why, what in the devil's name—?

ASLAKSEN: May I ask—isn't your father-in-law going about the town buying up all the Bath stock?

DR. STOCKMANN: Yes, he has been buying Bath stock to-day but—

ASLAKSEN: It would have been more prudent to let somebody else do that—some one not so closely connected with you.

HOVSTAD: And then you ought not to have appeared in the matter under your own name. No one need have known that the attack on the Baths came from you. You should have taken me into your counsel, Dr. Stockmann.

DR. STOCKMANN: [*Stares straight in front of him; a light seems to break in upon him, and he says as though thunderstruck.*] Is this possible? Can such things be?

ASLAKSEN: [*Smiling.*] It's plain enough that they can. But they ought to be managed delicately, you understand.

HOVSTAD: And there ought to be more people in it; for the responsibility always falls more lightly when there are several to share it.

DR. STOCKMANN: [*Calmly.*] In one word, gentlemen—what is it you want?

ASLAKSEN: Mr. Hovstad can best—

HOVSTAD: No, you explain, Aslaksen.

ASLAKSEN: Well, it's this: now that we know how the matter really stands, we believe we can venture to place the *People's Messenger* at your disposal.

DR. STOCKMANN: You can venture to now, eh? But how about public opinion? Aren't you afraid of bringing down a storm upon us?

HOVSTAD: We must manage to ride out the storm.

ASLAKSEN: And you must be ready to put about quickly, Doctor. As soon as your attack has done its work—

DR. STOCKMANN: As soon as my father-in-law and I have bought up the shares at a discount, you mean?

HOVSTAD: I presume it is mainly on scientific grounds that you want to take the management of the Baths into your own hands.

DR. STOCKMANN: Of course; it was on scientific grounds that I got the old Badger to stand in with me. And then we'll tinker up the water-Works a little, and potter about a bit down at the beach, without its costing the town sixpence. That ought to do the business Eh?

HOVSTAD: I think so—if you have the *Messenger* to back you up.

ASLAKSEN: In a free community the press is a power, Doctor.

DR. STOCKMANN: Yes, indeed; and so is public opinion. And you, Mr. Aslaksen—I suppose you will answer for the House-owners' Association?

ASLAKSEN: Both for the House-owners' Association and the Temperance Society. You may make your mind easy.

DR. STOCKMANN: But, gentlemen—really I'm quite ashamed to mention such a thing—but—what return—?

HOVSTAD: Of course, we should prefer to give you our support for nothing. But the *Messenger* is not very firmly established; it's not getting on as it ought to; and I should be very sorry to have to stop the paper just now, when there's so much to be done in general politics.

DR. STOCKMANN: Naturally; that would be very hard for a friend of the people like you. [*Flaring up.*] But I—I am

an enemy of the people! [*Striding about the room.*]
Where's my stick? Where the devil is my stick?

HOVSTAD: What do you mean?

ASLAKSEN: Surely you wouldn't—

DR. STOCKMANN: [*Standing still.*] And suppose I don't give
you a single farthing out of all my shares? You must
remember we rich folk don't like parting with our money.

HOVSTAD: And you must remember that this business of the
shares can be represented in two ways.

DR. STOCKMANN: Yes, you are the man for that; if I don't
come to the rescue of the *Messenger*, you'll manage to
put a vile complexion on the affair; you'll hunt me down,
I suppose—bait me—try to throttle me as a dog throttles
a hare!

HOVSTAD: That's a law of nature—every animal fights for its
own subsistence.

ASLAKSEN: And must take its food where it can find it, you
know.

DR. STOCKMANN: Then see if you can't find some out in the
gutter; [*Striding about the room.*] for now, by heaven! we
shall see which is the strongest animal of us three.
[*Finds his umbrella and brandishes it.*] Now, look here—!

HOVSTAD: You surely don't mean to assault us!

ASLAKSEN: I say, be careful with that umbrella!

DR. STOCKMANN: Out at the window with you, Mr. Hovstad!

HOVSTAD: [*By the hall door.*] Are you utterly crazy?

DR. STOCKMANN: Out at the window, Mr. Aslaksen! Jump I
tell you! Be quick about it!

ASLAKSEN: [*Running round the writing-table.*] Moderation,
Doctor; I'm not at all strong; I can't stand much—
[*Screams.*] Help! help!

Interpretation

1. What emotions do each of the three men feel as the dialogue
progresses? What changes occur in their attitudes? How can
these be reflected through tone of voice?

2. What feelings do you think Stockmann has for the two other men? How do they feel about him? How can this be shown through actions or movement?

3. Stockmann seems to be playing with Hovstad and Aslaksen before threatening them. How can this be made clear for an audience?

4. What lines prove that Hovstad and Aslaksen are dishonest and unethical? How can these lines be pointed up?

5. The two other men are afraid of Stockmann at the end. How can this be shown through a change in their placement?

6. You need to be careful not to make the ending seem slapstick. How can you present it seriously?

BliThe SpiriT

Noel Coward

Elvira, the ghost of his first wife, appeared to Charles the previous night, but no one else is able to see or hear her. Until the end of this scene Ruth refuses to believe that Charles actually sees his first wife. Elvira is different from what we would expect of a ghost. Rather than being commanding or fearsome, she merely is exasperating. The spirit world hasn't changed her; she's much as she probably was in life—petty and quarrelsome. (See page 33 for further background.)

This scene takes place at about 9:30 A.M. Charles has just joined Ruth who is having coffee and reading the newspaper. Elvira, who has been outside in the flower garden, now has come indoors.

CHARLES: Ruth, I want to explain to you clearly and without emotion that beyond any shadow of doubt the ghost or shade or whatever you like to call it of my first wife Elvira is in this room now.

RUTH: Yes, dear.

CHARLES: I know you don't believe it and are trying valiantly to humour me but I intend to prove it to you.

RUTH: Why not lie down and have a nice rest and you can prove anything you want later on?

CHARLES: She may not be here later on.

ELVIRA: Don't worry—she will!

CHARLES: O God!

RUTH: Hush, dear.

CHARLES: [*to* ELVIRA] Promise you'll do what I ask?

ELVIRA: That all depends what it is.

CHARLES: Ruth—you see that bowl of flowers on the piano?

RUTH: Yes, dear—I did it myself this morning.

ELVIRA: Very untidily if I may say so.

CHARLES: You may not.

RUTH: Very well—I never will again—I promise.

CHARLES: Elvira will now carry that bowl of flowers to the mantelpiece and back again. You will, Elvira, won't you—just to please me?

ELVIRA: I don't really see why I should—you've been quite insufferable to me ever since I materialized.

CHARLES: Please.

ELVIRA: All right, I will just this once—not that I approve of all these Herman The Great[1] carryings on. [*She goes over to the piano.*]

CHARLES: Now, Ruth—watch carefully.

RUTH: [*patiently*] Very well, dear.

CHARLES: Go on, Elvira—bring it to the mantelpiece and back again.

[ELVIRA *does so, taking obvious pleasure in doing it in a very roundabout way. At one moment she brings it up to within an inch of* RUTH'S *face.* RUTH *shrinks back with a scream and then jumps to her feet.*]

RUTH: [*furiously*] How dare you, Charles! You ought to be ashamed of yourself!

CHARLES: What on earth for?

RUTH: [*hysterically*] It's a trick—I know perfectly well it's a trick—you've been working up to this—it's all part of some horrible plan—

CHARLES: It isn't—I swear it isn't—Elvira—do something else for God's sake—

[1]A famous magician, Felix Herman, who died in 1938.

ELVIRA: Certainly—anything to oblige.

RUTH: [*becoming really frightened*] You want to get rid of me —you're trying to drive me out of my mind—

CHARLES: Don't be so silly.

RUTH: You're cruel and sadistic and I'll never forgive you— [ELVIRA *lifts up a light chair and waltzes solemnly round the room with it, then she puts it down with a bang. Making a dive for the door*] I'm not going to put up with this any more.

CHARLES: [*holding her*] You must believe it—you must—

RUTH: Let me go immediately.—

CHARLES: That was Elvira—I swear it was—

RUTH: [*struggling*] Let me go—

CHARLES: Ruth—please—

[RUTH *breaks away from him and runs toward the windows.* ELVIRA *gets there just before her and shuts them in her face.* RUTH *starts back, appalled.*

RUTH: [*looking at* CHARLES *with eyes of horror*] Charles—this is madness—sheer madness! It's some sort of auto-suggestion, isn't it—some form of hypnotism, swear to me it's only that? Swear to me it's only that.

ELVIRA: [*taking an expensive vase from the mantelpiece and crashing it into the grate*] Hypnotism, my foot!

[RUTH *gives a scream and goes into violent hysterics as the curtain falls.*]

Interpretation

1. What is Ruth's reaction to Charles's statement that Elvira is present? What does the line, "Yes, dear," imply? What tone of voice should you use in delivering this line?

2. How might you convey Charles's determination to prove that Elvira is present? What particular line first shows this determination.

3. It's apparent that Ruth has decided to humor Charles. Which line after "Yes, dear," shows this? Why do you think she has

decided to take this approach? Do you think this is logical? Illogical? Why?

4. Elvira is, of course, being disagreeable. What is the first line that shows this? Why do you think she is acting in this manner? How would you deliver the line to convey her feelings?

5. Pantomine or physical actions are very important in this scene. What emotions would you convey in the short segment where Elvira brings the flowers to Ruth? Why do you think Elvira is enjoying herself here? What facial expressions or actions might you use to show this? Ruth, of course, is frightened. Besides the directions given in the scene, what actions or sounds could you use to communicate the fright to an audience? What might Charles be doing?

6. What do the dashes indicate in Charles's speech that begins: "It isn't—I swear it isn't—Elvira . . ." What emotions do you think he is feeling here? How might you show these emotions?

7. The stage directions say that Ruth becomes "really frightened." Why is this so? How, through the use of your voice, could you show this intensification of her fright?

8. The scene builds in intensity from beginning to end. Elvira becomes more determined and more spiteful in trying to frighten Ruth, who, in turn, does become more frantic. Charles then becomes more upset at what is happening. Yet, the actions must be controlled or the audience will have no point of focus. From Charles's line: "What on earth for?" to the end of the scene, determine who should be the point of focus on each line. Then figure out how this can be done.

No Exit

Jean-Paul Sartre

The three principal characters in this play are confined to a one room apartment in hell. According to the stage directions, the room is decorated in "Second Empire style," which means it is a highly decorative imitation of earlier styles. Each character is trying to change or relive his or her earthly life.

The play is largely a way for Sartre to express his belief in existentialism, a philosophy concerned with responsible freedom. Existentialists believe that individuals are completely responsible for their actions. One's actions make one's self. Life has meaning and purpose only insofar as individuals create it for themselves. Existentialists believe that individuals ought to live their lives as if there were no social pressure. In other words, a person is essentially so alone that other people do not really matter.

The play contains the famous line: "Hell is other people." In the context of the play this means that characters are no longer in charge of their lives but are affected by the world outside of themselves. Thus they lose their freedom and create a hell for themselves.

The two women and one man, each with sordid pasts, find they are interdependent on their triangular relationship, despite differences in background. In effect, each discovers that in life or death indifference is impossible.

INEZ: You're very pretty. I wish we'd had some flowers to welcome you with.

ESTELLE: Flowers? Yes, I loved flowers. Only they'd fade so quickly here, wouldn't they? It's so stuffy. Oh, well, the great thing is to keep as cheerful as we can, don't you agree? Of course, you, too, are—

INEZ: Yes. Last week. What about you?

ESTELLE: I'm—quite recent. Yesterday. As a matter of fact, the ceremony's not quite over. [*Her tone is natural enough, but she seems to be seeing what she describes.*] The wind's blowing my sister's veil all over the place. She's trying her best to cry. Come, dear! Make another effort. That's better. Two tears, two little tears are twinkling under the black veil. Oh dear! What a sight Olga looks this morning! She's holding my sister's arm, helping her along. She's not crying, and I don't blame her; tears always mess one's face up, don't they? Olga was my bosom friend, you know.

INEZ: Did you suffer much?

ESTELLE: No. I was only half conscious, mostly.

INEZ: What was it?

ESTELLE: Pneumonia. [*In the same tone as before.*] It's over now, they're leaving the cemetery. Good-by. Good-by. Quite a crowd they are. My husband's stayed at home. Prostrated with grief, poor man. [*To* INEZ] How about you?

INEZ: The gas stove.

ESTELLE: And you, Mr. Garcin?

GARCIN: Twelve bullets through my chest. [ESTELLE *makes a horrified gesture.*] Sorry! I fear I'm not good company for the dead.

ESTELLE: Please, please don't use that word. It's so— so crude. In terribly bad taste, really. It doesn't mean much, anyhow. Somehow I feel we've never been so much alive as now. If we've absolutely got to mention this—this state of things, I suggest we call ourselves—wait!—absentees. Have you been—been absent for long?

GARCIN: About a month.

ESTELLE: Where do you come from?

GARCIN: From Rio.

ESTELLE: I'm from Paris. Have you anyone left down there?

GARCIN: Yes, my wife. [*In the same tone as* ESTELLE *has been using.*] She's waiting at the entrance of the barracks. She comes there every day. But they won't let her in. Now she's trying to peep between the bars. She doesn't yet know I'm—absent, but she suspects it. Now she's going away. She's wearing her black dress. So much the better, she won't need to change. She isn't crying, but she never did cry, anyhow. It's a bright sunny day and she's like a black shadow creeping down the empty street. Those big tragic eyes of hers—with that martyred look they always had. Oh, how she got on my nerves!

[*A short silence.* GARCIN *sits on the central sofa and buries his head in his hands.*]

INEZ: Estelle!

ESTELLE: Please, Mr. Garcin!

GARCIN: What is it?

ESTELLE: You're sitting on my sofa.

GARCIN: I beg your pardon. [*He gets up.*]

ESTELLE: You looked so—so far away. Sorry I disturbed you.

GARCIN: I was setting my life in order. [INEZ *starts laughing.*] You may laugh, but you'd do better to follow my example.

INEZ: No need. My life's in perfect order. It tidied itself up nicely of its own accord. So I needn't bother about it now.

GARCIN: Really? You imagine it's so simple as that. [*He runs his hand over his forehead*] Whew! How hot it is here! Do you mind if—? [*He begins taking off his coat.*]

ESTELLE: How dare you! [*More gently*] No, please don't. I loathe men in their shirt-sleeves.

GARCIN: [*Putting on his coat again*] All right. [*A short pause*] Of course I used to spend my nights in the newspaper office, and it was a regular Black Hole, so we never kept our coats on. Stiflingly hot it could be. [*Short pause. In the same tone as previously.*] Stifling that it *is.* It's night now.

ESTELLE: That's so. Olga's undressing; it must be after midnight. How quickly the time passes, on earth!

INEZ: Yes, after midnight. They've sealed up my room. It's dark, pitch-dark, and empty.

Interpretation

1. This scene occurs near the beginning of the play. What sort of relationships do you see being established among the three characters? How can you show this through placement?

2. Estelle is being somewhat sarcastic about people's reactions to her death. What lines show this? How can the sarcasm be conveyed through her voice?

3. How does Estelle feel about her husband? What tone of voice would be logical for her to use in reference to him?

4. Garcin, like Estelle, mocks his spouse's reaction to his death. What tone of voice could he use to convey his feelings? What posture?

5. Why does Estelle say that Garcin is so far away? What is he feeling? How can this be shown?

6. Inez doesn't want to think or talk about her life on earth. What emotions could she be feeling? How could they be pointed up?

7. Inez reacts pretty matter-of-factly to her death. We can only surmise why. Perhaps it's too painful to discuss or think about or maybe it really is of little concern. How might you vocally convey her matter-of-factness?

Scenes for Mixed Groups

Barefoot in the Park

An Enemy of the People

The Bald Soprano

West Side Story

Act 2, scene 2

Barefoot in the Park

Neil Simon

T he two main characters, Paul and Corie, are recently married and are learning to adjust to each other. And that's
where the problem lies. Paul, a young lawyer, is used to a
conservative lifestyle, while Corie is adventurous and willing to
experiment with new things. Neither is willing to compromise.
The other two major characters parallel Paul and Corie, only
they are older. Corie's mother is a "stick-in-the-mud" like Paul,
and Velasco, a neighbor, is lively and adventurous. The play, of
course, is a comedy that deals with the problems of adjusting to
people and situations. Each character learns to compromise and
to give a bit of self to a relationship if it's to be worthwhile.

In this scene the four characters have returned home after a
night on the town. There is a long climb to the studio apartment
where the young couple lives.

MOTHER: [*Finally.*] . . . I feel like we've died . . . and gone to
heaven . . . only we had to climb up . . . .

PAUL: [*Gathering his strength.*] . . . Struck down in the
prime of life . . . .

MOTHER: . . . I don't really feel sick . . . Just kind of numb
. . . and I can't make a fist . . . [*She holds up a stiff
hand.*]

PAUL: You want to hear something frightening? . . . My
teeth feel soft . . . It's funny . . . but the best thing we
had all night was the knichi.

MOTHER: Anyway, Corie had a good time . . . Don't you think
Corie had a good time, Paul?

PAUL: [*Struggling up onto the couch.*] Wonderful . . . Poor kid . . . It isn't often we get out to Staten Island in February.

MOTHER: She seems to get such a terrific kick out of living. You've got to admire that, don't you, Paul?

PAUL: I admire anyone who has three portions of poofla-poo pie.

MOTHER: [*Starts.*] What's poofla-poo pie?

PAUL: Don't you remember? That gook that came in a turban.

MOTHER: I thought that was the waiter . . . . I tried, Paul. But I just couldn't seem to work up an appetite the way they did.

PAUL: [*Reassuring her.*] No, no, Mom . . . You mustn't blame yourself . . . . We're just not used to that kind of food . . . . You just don't pick up your fork and dig into a *brown* salad . . . . You've got to play around with it for a while.

MOTHER: Maybe I *am* getting old . . . . I don't mind telling you it's very discouraging . . . . [*With great difficulty, she manages to rouse herself and get up from the couch.*] Anyway, I don't think I could get through coffee . . . . I'm all out of pink pills . . . .

PAUL: Where are you going?

MOTHER: Home . . . I want to die in my own bed. [*Exhausted, she sinks into a chair.*]

PAUL: Well, what'll I tell them?

MOTHER: Oh, make up some clever little lie. [*She rallies herself and gets up.*] Tell Corie I'm not really her mother. She'll probably never want to see me again anyway . . . Good night, dear. [*Just as* MOTHER *gets to the door, it opens and* CORIE *and* VELASCO *return.*] Oh, coffee ready? [*She turns back into the room.* VELASCO *crosses to the bar as* CORIE *moves to behind the couch.*]

CORIE: I was whistling the Armenian National Anthem and I blew out the pilot light.

VELASCO: [*Puts four brandy snifters he has brought in down on the bar, and taking a decanter from the bar begins to pour brandy.*] Instead we're going to have a flaming brandy . . . Corie, give everyone a match.

[CORIE *moves to the side table.*]

MOTHER: I'm afraid you'll have to excuse me, dear. It *is* a little late.

CORIE: [*Moves toward* MOTHER] Mother, you're not going home. It's the shank of the evening.

MOTHER: I know, but I've got a ten-o'clock dentist appointment . . . at nine o'clock . . . and it's been a very long evening . . . . What I mean is it's late, but I've had a wonderful time . . . . I don't know what I'm saying.

CORIE: But, Mother . . . .

MOTHER: Darling, I'll call you in the morning. Good night, Paul . . . Good night, Mr. Velasco . . . .

VELASCO: [*Putting down the brandy, he crosses to* CORIE] Good night, Paul . . . Good night, Corie . . . .

CORIE: Mr. Velasco, you're not going, too?

VELASCO: [*Taking his beret and scarf from* CORIE *and putting them on.*] Of course. I'm driving Mrs. Banks home.

MOTHER: [*Moves away in shock.*] *Oh, no!* . . . [*She recovers herself and turns back.*] I mean, oh, no, it's too late.

VELASCO: [*To* MOTHER.] Too late for what?

MOTHER: The buses. They stop running at two. How will you get home?

VELASCO: Why worry about it now? I'll meet that problem in New Jersey.

[VELASCO *moves to the door and* CORIE *in great jubilation flings herself over the back of the couch.*]

MOTHER: And it's such a long trip . . . . [*She crosses to* CORIE.] Corie, isn't it a long trip?

CORIE: Not really. It's only about thirty minutes.

MOTHER: But it's such an inconvenience. Really, Mr. Velasco, it's very sweet of you but—

VELASCO: Victor!

MOTHER: What?

VELASCO: If we're going to spend the rest of the evening together, it must be Victor.

MOTHER: Oh!

VELASCO: And I insist the arrangement be reciprocal. What is it?

MOTHER: What is what?

CORIE: Your name, Mother. [*To* VELASCO.] It's Ethel.

MOTHER: Oh, that's right. Ethel. My name is Ethel.

VELASCO: That's better . . . . Now . . . are we ready . . . Ethel?

MOTHER: Well . . . if you insist, Walter.

VELASCO: Victor! It's Victor.

MOTHER: Yes. Victor!

VELASCO: Good night, Paul . . . Shama shama, Corie.

CORIE: Shama shama!

VELASCO: [*Moves to the door.*] If you don't hear from us in a week, we'll be at the Nacional Hotel in Mexico City . . . . Room seven-oh-three! . . . Let's go, Ethel! [*And he goes out the door.* MOTHER *turns to* CORIE *and looks for help.*]

MOTHER: [*Frightened, she grabs* CORIE'S *arm.*] What does he mean by that?

CORIE: I don't know, but I'm dying to find out. Will you call me in the morning?

MOTHER: Yes . . . about six o'clock! [*And in a panic, she exits.*]

Interpretation

1. In this scene what parallels can you find between Paul and Ethel? Between Corie and Velasco? How can their similarities be emphasized for an audience?

2. How do Ethel and Paul feel about each other in this scene? How could tone of voice make this clearer for an audience?

3. Pick out the speeches that have punch lines or phrases that should be emphasized for a laugh. How can you emphasize them?

4. How do Corie and Velasco feel about each other? Find the lines that show this. How can the lines be presented so the audience understands the feelings?

5. How does Ethel react emotionally to Velasco's plan to see her home? How can this be pointed up through her voice?

6. What emotion does Corie feel at the end of the scene? How can this be presented effectively to an audience?

Act 5

An Enemy of the People

Henrik Ibsen

In this scene Dr. Stockmann receives the news about the baths he has been awaiting. The water sample he sent away to be analyzed is highly contaminated. As you learned earlier, the baths provide much of the town's income. (See p. 128 for further background.) This scene occurs in the Stockmann house shortly after the beginning of the play. Dr. Stockmann's brother, Peter, the Burgomaster (a town official) has just left after criticizing his brother's lifestyle: he spends too much money on household items, eats unnecessary foods, and so forth. Thus the audience knows that one of Dr. Stockmann's strongest opponents in the argument over whether or not to close the baths will be the Burgomaster.

DR. STOCKMANN: [*Flourishing the letter.*] Here's news, I can tell you, that will waken up the town!

BILLING: News?

MRS. STOCKMANN: What news?

DR. STOCKMANN: A great discovery, Katrina!

HOVSTAD: Indeed?

MRS. STOCKMANN: Made by you?

DR. STOCKMANN: Precisely—by me! [*Walks up and down.*] Now let them go on accusing me of fads and crack-brained notions. But they won't dare to! Ha-ha! I tell you they won't dare!

PETRA: Do tell us what it is, father.

DR. STOCKMANN: Well, well, give me time, and you shall hear all about it. If only I had Peter here now! This just shows how we men can go about forming judgments like the blindest moles—

HOVSTAD: What do you mean, doctor?

DR. STOCKMANN: [*Stopping beside the table.*] Isn't it the general opinion that our town is a healthy place?

HOVSTAD: Of course.

DR. STOCKMANN: A quite exceptionally healthy place, indeed— a place to be warmly recommended, both to invalids and people in health.

MRS. STOCKMANN: My dear Thomas—

DR. STOCKMANN: And assuredly we haven't failed to recommend and belaud it. I've sung its praises again and again, both in the *Messenger* and in pamphlets—

HOVSTAD: Well, what then?

DR. STOCKMANN: These Baths, that we have called the pulse of the town, its vital nerve, and—and the devil knows what else—

BILLING: "Our city's palpitating heart," I once ventured to call them in a convivial moment—

DR. STOCKMANN: Yes, I daresay. Well—do you know what they really are, these mighty, magnificent, belauded Baths, that have cost so much money—do you know what they are?

HOVSTAD: No, what are they?

MRS. STOCKMANN: Do tell us.

DR. STOCKMANN: Simply a pestiferous hole, carrying or spreading infectious disease.

PETRA: The Baths, father?

MRS. STOCKMANN: [*At the same time.*] Our Baths!

HOVSTAD: [*Also at the same time.*] But, Doctor—!

BILLING: Oh, it's incredible!

DR. STOCKMANN: I tell you the whole place is a poisonous whited-sepulchre; noxious in the highest degree! All that filth up there in the Mill Dale—the stuff that smells so horribly—taints the water in the feedpipes of the Pump-Room; and the same accursed poisonous refuse oozes out by the beach—

HOVSTAD: Where the sea-baths are?

DR. STOCKMANN: Exactly.

HOVSTAD: But how are you so sure of all this, Doctor?

DR. STOCKMANN: I've investigated the whole thing as conscientiously as possible. I've long had my suspicions about it. Last year we had some extraordinary cases of illness among the patients—both typhoid and gastric attacks—

MRS. STOCKMANN: Yes, I remember.

DR. STOCKMANN: We thought at the time that the visitors had brought the infection with them; but afterwards—last winter—I began to question that. So I set about testing the water as well as I could.

MRS. STOCKMANN: It was that you were working so hard at!

DR. STOCKMANN: Yes, you may well say I've worked, Katrina. But here, you know, I hadn't the necessary scientific appliances; so I sent samples both of our drinking water and of our sea-water to the University, for exact analysis by a chemist.

HOVSTAD: And you have received his report?

DR. STOCKMANN: [*Showing letter.*] Here it is! And it proves beyond dispute the presence of putrefying organic matter in the water—millions of infusoria. It's absolutely pernicious to health, whether used internally or externally.

MRS. STOCKMANN: What a blessing you found it out in time.

DR. STOCKMANN: Yes, you may well say that.

HOVSTAD: And what do you intend to do now, Doctor?

DR. STOCKMANN: Why, to set things right, of course.

HOVSTAD: You think it can be done, then?

DR. STOCKMANN: It must be done. Else the whole Baths are useless, ruined. But there's no fear. I am quite clear as to what is required.

MRS. STOCKMANN: But, my dear Thomas, why should you have made such a secret of all this?

DR. STOCKMANN: Would you have had me rush all over the town and chatter about it, before I was quite certain? No, thank you; I'm not so mad as that.

PETRA: But to us at home—

DR. STOCKMANN: I couldn't say a word to a living soul. But to-morrow you may look in at the Badger's—

MRS. STOCKMANN: Oh, Thomas!

DR. STOCKMANN: Well, well, at your grandfather's. The old fellow will be astonished! He thinks I'm not quite right in my head—yes, and plenty of others think the same, I've noticed. But now these good people shall see—yes, they shall see now! [*Walks up and down rubbing his hands.*] What a stir there will be in the town, Katrina! Just think of it! All the water pipes will have to be relaid.

HOVSTAD: [*Rising.*] All the water pipes—?

DR. STOCKMANN: Why, of course. The intake is too low down; it must be moved much higher up.

PETRA: So you were right, after all?

DR. STOCKMANN: Yes, do you remember, Petra? I wrote against it when they were beginning the works. But no one would listen to me then. Now, you may be sure, I shall give them my full broadside—for of course I've prepared a statement for the Directors; it has been lying ready a whole week; I've only been waiting for this report. [*Points to letter.*] But now they shall have it at once. [*Goes into his room and returns with a MS. in his hand.*] See! Four closely-written sheets! And I'll enclose the report. A newspaper, Katrina! Get me something to wrap them up in. There—that's it. Give it to—to—[*Stamps.*] what the devil's her name? Give it to the girl, I mean, and tell her to take it at once to the Burgomaster.

[MRS. STOCKMANN *goes out with the packet through the dining-room.*]

PETRA: What do you think Uncle Peter will say, father?

DR. STOCKMANN: What should he say? He can't possibly be otherwise than pleased that so important a fact has been brought to light.

HOVSTAD: I suppose you will let me put a short announcement of your discovery in the *Messenger*.

DR. STOCKMANN: Yes, I shall be much obliged if you will.

HOVSTAD: It is highly desirable that the public should know about it as soon as possible.

DR. STOCKMANN: Yes, certainly.

MRS. STOCKMANN: [*Returning.*] She's gone with it.

BILLING: Strike me dead if you won't be the first man in the town, Doctor!

DR. STOCKMANN: [*Walks up and down in high glee.*] Oh, nonsense! After all, I have done no more than my duty. I've been a lucky treasure-hunter, that's all. But all the same—

BILLING: Hovstad, don't you think the town ought to get up a torchlight procession in honour of Dr. Stockmann?

HOVSTAD: I shall certainly propose it.

BILLING: And I'll talk it over with Aslaksen.

DR. STOCKMANN: No, my dear friends; let all such claptrap alone. I won't hear of anything of the sort. And if the Directors should want to raise my salary, I won't accept it. I tell you, Katrina, I will not accept it.

MRS. STOCKMANN: You are quite right, Thomas.

PETRA: [*Raising her glass.*] Your health, father!

HOVSTAD *and* BILLING: Your health, your health, Doctor!

HORSTER: [*Clinking glasses with the* DOCTOR.] I hope you may have nothing but joy of your discovery.

DR. STOCKMANN: Thanks, thanks, my dear friends! I can't tell you how happy I am—! Oh, what a blessing it is to feel that you have deserved well of your native town and your fellow citizens. Hurrah, Katrina!

[*He puts both his arms round her neck, and whirls her round with him.* MRS. STOCKMANN *screams and struggles. A burst of laughter, applause, and cheers for the* DOCTOR. *The boys thrust their heads in at the door.*]

Interpretation

1. Who is the dominant character in this scene? How can this be shown through physical arrangement?

2. What emotions does Dr. Stockmann feel when he receives the news about the water analysis? How can this be emphasized through tone of voice?

3. Hovstad is impatient to hear what Dr. Stockmann has found out. How can his impatience be shown through movement or gesture?

4. How does each character react to the news? How can this be pointed up for an audience?

The Bald Soprano

Eugene Ionesco

I n this scene the Martins have come to visit the Smiths, after either having been expected or not expected. The audience doesn't know which is correct because many of the things the characters say are contradicted, and the play has no logical progression of events. The point is that much of life is absurd and that people really don't pay attention to what others say. As in the opening scene on page 9, the author is showing us that people often are so self-centered that they pay little attention to what others tell them.

MR. SMITH: Hm. [*Silence.*]

MRS. SMITH: Hm, hm. [*Silence.*]

MRS. MARTIN: Hm, hm, hm. [*Silence.*]

MR. MARTIN: Hm, hm, hm, hm. [*Silence.*]

MRS. MARTIN: Oh, but definitely. [*Silence.*]

MR. MARTIN: We all have colds. [*Silence.*]

MR. SMITH: Nevertheless, it's not chilly. [*Silence.*]

MRS. SMITH: There's no draft. [*Silence.*]

MR. MARTIN: Oh no, fortunately. [*Silence.*]

MR. SMITH: Oh dear, oh dear, oh dear. [*Silence.*]

MR. MARTIN: Don't you feel well? [*Silence.*]

MRS. SMITH: No, he's wet his pants. [*Silence.*]

MRS. MARTIN: Oh, sir, at your age, you shouldn't. [*Silence.*]

MR. SMITH: The heart is ageless. [*Silence.*]

MR. MARTIN: That's true. [*Silence.*]

MRS. SMITH: So they say. [*Silence.*]

MRS. MARTIN: They also say the opposite. [*Silence.*]

MR. SMITH: The truth lies somewhere between the two. [*Silence.*]

MR. MARTIN: That's true. [*Silence.*]

MRS. SMITH: [*to the Martins*]: Since you travel so much, you must have many interesting things to tell us.

MR. MARTIN [*to his wife*]: My dear, tell us what you've seen today.

MRS. MARTIN: It's scarcely worth the trouble, for no one would believe me.

MR. SMITH: We're not going to question your sincerity!

MRS. SMITH: You will offend us if you think that.

MR. MARTIN [*to his wife*]: You will offend them, my dear, if you think that . . .

MRS. MARTIN [*graciously*]: Oh well, today I witnessed something extraordinary. Something really incredible.

MR. MARTIN: Tell us quickly, my dear.

MR. SMITH: Oh, this is going to be amusing.

MRS. SMITH: At last.

MRS. MARTIN: Well, today, when I went shopping to buy some vegetables, which are getting to be dearer and dearer . . .

MRS. SMITH: Where is it all going to end!

MR. SMITH: You shouldn't interrupt, my dear, it's very rude.

MRS. MARTIN: In the street, near a cafe, I saw a man, properly dressed, about fifty years old, or not even that, who . . .

MR. SMITH: Who, what?

MRS. SMITH: Who, what?

MR. SMITH [*to his wife*]: Don't interrupt, my dear, you're disgusting.

MRS. SMITH: My dear, it is you who interrupted first, you boor.

MR. SMITH [*to his wife*]: Hush. [*To Mrs. Martin*]: What was this man doing?

MRS. MARTIN: Well, I'm sure you'll say that I'm making it up
—He was down on one knee and he was bent over.

MR. MARTIN, MR. SMITH, MRS. SMITH: Oh!

MRS. MARTIN: Yes, bent over.

MR. SMITH: Not possible.

MRS. MARTIN: Yes, bent over. I went near him to see what
he was doing . . .

MR. SMITH: And?

MRS. MARTIN: He was tying his shoe lace which had come
undone.

MR. MARTIN, MR. SMITH, MRS. SMITH: Fantastic!

MR. SMITH: If someone else had told me this, I'd not believe
it.

MR. MARTIN: Why not? One sees things even more extraordinary every day, when one walks around. For
instance, today in the Underground I myself saw a man,
quietly sitting on a seat, reading his newspaper.

MRS. SMITH: What a character!

Interpretation

1. Mrs. Smith says, "We all have colds." What lines contradict
this? State two other contradictions you find in the scene. How
can these lines be delivered?

2. What tone of voice do you think would be appropriate for the
characters to use throughout the scene? Why?

3. What absurdities of life does Ionesco point out in this scene?
How can these absurdities be emphasized for an audience?

4. What are the relationships like between Mr. and Mrs. Smith
and between Mr. and Mrs. Martin? How can the character of the
relationships be shown through action or voice?

5. Silence is indicated in the stage directions after each of the first few lines. How during the silence can you show the characters' reactions to what is happening?

6. After the silences end, the characters indicate they feel differently. How can you communicate these new reactions?

7. How do the Smiths and the Martins feel about each other? How can you show these feelings?

8. How can you maintain audience interest in this scene through movement, placement, and voice?

Act 1, scene 5

West Side Story

Laurents, Bernstein and Sondheim

As you learned earlier, this musical, one of the most popular ever written, concerns the clash between two different cultures, the Jets, an American street gang, and the Sharks, a street gang made up of teenagers from Puerto Rico. (See p. 111 for further background.)

In this scene the Puerto Rican teenagers discuss, often sarcastically, the differences between life in New York City and life in Puerto Rico and their responses to the differences. You may choose to present the scene either with or without the song.

BERNARDO: [*Looking up to the window.*] Maria?

ANITA: She *has* a mother. Also a father.

BERNARDO: They do not know this country any better than she does.

ANITA: You do not know it at all! Girls here are free to have fun. She-is-in-America-now.

BERNARDO: [*exaggerated*] But Puerto-Rico-is-in-America-now!

ANITA: [*in disgust*] Ai!

BERNARDO: [*cooing*] Anita Josefina Teresita—

ANITA: It's plain Anita now—

BERNARDO: [*continuing through*]—Beatriz del Carmen Margarita, etcetera, etcetera—

ANITA: Immigrant!

BERNARDO: [*pulling her to him*] Thank God, you can't change your hair!

PEPE: [*fondling* CONSUELO'S *bleached mop*] Is that possible?

CONSUELO: In the U.S.A., everything is real.

BERNARDO: [*to* CHINO, *who enters*] Chino, how was she when you took her home?

CHINO: All right. 'Nardo, she was only dancing.

BERNARDO: With an *"American."* Who is really a Polack.

ANITA: Says the Spic.

BERNARDO: You are not so cute.

ANITA: That Tony is.

ROSALIA: And he works.

CHINO: A delivery boy.

ANITA: And what are you?

CHINO: An assistant.

BERNARDO: *Si!* And Chino makes half what the Polack makes —the Polack is American!

ANITA: Ai! Here comes the whole commercial! [*A burlesque oration in mock Puerto Rican accent.* BERNARDO *starts the first line with her.*] The mother of Tony was born in Poland; the father still goes to night school. Tony was born in America, so that makes him an American. But us? Foreigners!

PEPE AND CONSUELO: Lice!

PEPE, CONSUELO, ANITA: Cockroaches!

BERNARDO: Well, it is true! You remember how we were when we first came! Did we even think of going back?

BERNARDO AND ANITA: No! We came ready, eager—

ANITA: [*mocking*] With our hearts open—

CONSUELO: Our arms open—

PEPE: You came with your pants open.

CONSUELO: *You* did, pig! [*Slaps him.*] You'll go back with handcuffs!

BERNARDO: I am going back with a Cadillac!

CHINO: Air-conditioned!

BERNARDO: Built-in bar!

CHINO: Telephone!

BERNARDO: Television!

CHINO: Compatible color!

BERNARDO: And a king-sized bed. [*Grabs* ANITA.] Come on.

ANITA: [*mimicking*] Come on.

BERNARDO: Well, are you or aren't you?

ANITA: Well, are you or aren't you?

BERNARDO: Well, are you?

ANITA: You have your big, important war council. The council or me?

BERNARDO: First one, then the other.

ANITA: [*breaking away from him*] I am an American girl now. I don't wait.

BERNARDO: [*to* CHINO] Back home, women know their place.

ANITA: Back home, little boys don't have war councils.

BERNARDO: You want me to be an American? [*To the boys.*] *Vámonos, chicos, es tarde.* [*A mock bow.*] *Buenas noches,* Anita Josefina del Carmen, etcetera, etcetera, etcetera.

[*He exits with the boys.*]

ROSALIA: That's a very pretty name: Etcetera.

ANITA: Ai!

CONSUELO: She means well.

ROSALIA: We have many pretty names at home.

ANITA: [*mimicking*] At home, at home. If it's so nice "at home," why don't you go back there?

ROSALIA: I would like to—[*A look from* ANITA]—just for a successful visit.
[*She sings nostalgically:*]
    Puerto Rico . . .
    You lovely island . . .
    Island of tropical breezes.
        Always the pineapples growing,
        Always the coffee blossoms blowing . . .

ANITA: [*sings sarcastically*]
Puerto Rico . . .
You ugly island . . .
Island of tropic diseases.
　Always the hurricanes blowing,
　Always the population growing . . .
　And the money owing,
　And the babies crying,
　And the bullets flying.
I like the island Manhattan—
Smoke on your pipe and put that in!

[*All, except* ROSALIA:]
　I like to be in America!
　OK by me in America!
　Everything free in America
　For a small fee in America!

ROSALIA: I like the city of San Juan—

ANITA: I know a boat you can get on.

ROSALIA: Hundreds of flowers in full bloom—

ANITA: Hundreds of people in each room!

[*All, except* ROSALIA:]
　Automobile in America,
　Chromium steel in America,
　Wire-spoke wheel in America—
　Very big deal in America!

ROSALIA: I'll drive a Buick through San Juan—

ANITA: If there's a road you can drive on.

ROSALIA: I'll give my cousins a free ride—

ANITA: How you get all of them inside?

[*All, except* ROSALIA:]
　Immigrant goes to America,
　Many hellos in America;
　Nobody knows in America
　Puerto Rico's in America.

[*The girls whistle and dance.*]

ROSALIA: When will I go back to San Juan—

ANITA: When will you shut up and get gone!

ROSALIA: I'll give them new washing machine—

ANITA: What have they got there to keep clean?

[*All, except* ROSALIA:]
I like the shores of America!
Comfort is yours in America!
Knobs on the door in America,
Wall-to-wall floors in America!

[*They whistle and dance.*]

ROSALIA: I'll bring a TV to San Juan—

ANITA: If there's a current to turn on.

ROSALIA: Everyone there will give big cheer!

ANITA: Everyone there will have moved here!

[*The song ends in the joyous dance.*]

The Lights Black Out.

Interpretation

1. How can you determine how the characters feel about America? About Puerto Rico? If so, what are they feeling? How can the feelings be communicated to an audience?

2. What is the predominant mood of this scene? How can it be communicated?

3. What differences can you see among the personalities of the characters in this scene? How can these be shown?

4. Bernardo and Anita are disagreeing. How do they feel about each other? How can they react physically to show this feeling?